Welcome Home Macho Man

Ernest Spencer

Published by Corps Productions, Inc
Walnut Creek, CA
Many thanks to:
Editor – Jana Doyle Hollenbeck
Cover Design – Paula Woolcott
Cover Sculpture Artist – Dennis Smith

Table of Contents

Dedication

TO MY FAMILY

My life has been a series of roles I played for others. It was not easy being a star. I played one for much of my life. You might find this statement presumptuous, but I was raised to act that way. I was cute, witty, funny, outrageous, and admired. I was always the center of attention. It seemed natural. But living one's life for others to the extent I did hurt me to my core.

I saw the world with naïve eyes. It took decades of tears, trials, and tribulations for me to realize I had been foolish. Being the center of attention was an empty, lonely role. I never had time to reflect upon what it was I wanted for myself. The praise was intoxicating, addicting. But like other things, it damages you if done in unhealthy ways.

My parents grew up during the "Great Depression." Dad's father Ernest supported his family in Rhode Island during this time by raising chickens for the "speakeasies." Prior to that my grandfather worked in the only textile mill in their hometown of Harrisville, Rhode Island. Textiles provided the bulk of the jobs in the Northeast United States at the time.

Before the depression, mom's parents owned a thriving laundry that served the military around Pearl Harbor. They washed, starched, and ironed the uniforms for soldiers and officers alike. My maternal grandmother had a box that had the insignias for officers from the rank of second lieutenant to general. When the depression came my mom's parents lost their business. They could not find work. Mom, unlike dad, endured a life of poverty.

Goods as they are called, are always subject to demand. The time before the depression saw excesses of almost every kind. Money is an illusion, created as a way to obtain things. My dad's father adapted by providing goods to places that still did business. Ernest delivered fully dressed chickens to the speakeasies around Providence. They were illegal, but grandpa didn't seem to mind.

Dad told me Grandpa Ernest was a horse thief. That's why he ran away from home in Rochester, New York. Ernest and my great grandparents had emigrated from England and settled there. Ernest was a man of few words and never talked about his past.

Speakeasies sold "bootleg" liquor. That term evolved from a way people hid the liquor. Righteous, well meaning, mostly women used protests and marches to change the law. Laws were passed to ban the sale and use of alcohol. Liquor seems to be prevalent in most cultures. Some societies use drugs. Both cause a mind-altering state.

I have lived long enough to see that things are not what we really need. We need love. Love cannot be bought. Love can only be given and shared.

PREFACE

My mindset from the time I was a child was to question everything. Why? "Why is there a moon mommy?" Mom reminds me of that incident when I had been a child of four. We stood together looking up into the night heavens outside our home in Kailua on the windward side of O'ahu. She does not remember much of the incident except that facet of me.

"You were always questioning everything, my son," she says, now frail and nearing the end of her life. "Oh, my son," she repeats once more staring forlornly at me as we sit in her final home in Ewa Beach. "Your mind was always outside yourself. You are a very unique, special person, my son. I wished you had gone down a different path in life. You were so innocent and loving, Ern."

"I knew no other way, mom. Look where it has gotten me," I say with no hint of the inner turmoil that possesses me.

I always look at things and wonder what they represent and mean more than what they are. I have lived a life of questioning. Near his end daddy says, "Ern, your mind was always churning, churning." He spins his small left arthritic crippled fist at me in demonstration. He can no longer sit fully upright. His body hunches over. He does not shake or move involuntarily. He holds his composure and breathes slowly.

"It is who I am daddy," I say softly as I take his hand in mine. "You made me who I am."

"No Ern. You were always your own person. I am proud of you, my son. Your father is proud of you." There is a slight watering and gleam that comes suddenly in his weary eyes. "I wish I could have been you." He looks away, seeming ashamed of what he just said. The raw honest truth from him stuns me.

"Why?" I look at him my mouth agape. He does not answer for some moments.

"You are and have always been a strong, brave, good man Ern. You are honest and care, my son. You really do care."

"Do I? How do you know who I really am daddy?" I let my words sit until he turns his gaze to me once again. I hold his attention with my stare. I feel my eyes penetrate his calm demeanor. He starts to speak, then stops. Finally. He takes a slow deep breath and speaks.

"I know much about you my son," he says. "It is a shitty world out there. Only men like you understand and care. Most people don't give a damn about anything except themselves."

"Well, lucky them." I say those words in anger. I am tired of always taking care of others. I live my life for the sake of others. I am tired of being that way. The habit is hard to break. Only the end of my third marriage makes me cognizant of what I need to do to live my dreams. I have been trapped in the role of being the giver, and hero for others. I yearn for the day when I can be who I want instead of what others want. I need to climb down off that dreadful pedestal my mother and others have placed me on.

LIFE BEFORE VIETNAM

My Earliest Recollections

My earliest recollections are of my mom and dad. They both profoundly affect who I become and how I act. Yes, act. They placed me upon a stage not of my own making. I cannot speculate who I might have been had I not been raised that way. It was their own selfish wants and dreams that made them guide me the way they did.

"Did I ever tell you my son that I was not supposed to have you?" This line my mom repeats endlessly towards the end of her life. Mom told and retold the tale of her having me deliberately, ignoring our family doctor's order not to have any more children after my brother was born.

Dr. Gaspar, our family doctor, delivered my brother and me. My brother is a difficult birth for my mom. She almost dies. Billy is born through the use of instruments, crude instruments. He is torn from my mother. His left arm withers as a result. Mom tries as much as she can to help him. He spends long periods of time in the free Shriner's Hospital only a block away from Maryknoll, where we eventually will go to school.

The Shriners, a men's club made up of the elite, built their own hospital to care for children who need medical help. They are the professionals of Hawai'i society. They practice experimental surgical techniques on their young wards. My brother is a guinea pig. What they do to his arm leaves it scarred and does nothing to give it anything of use. It always dangles at his side like a small broken wing. They are not enlightened in those days. Mom is only allowed to visit for one hour on Sunday. We have to take several buses, mom, my sister Betty, and me, to get there. It is often hot in the sun on many of those Sundays. My sister and I are only allowed into the hospital a few times to see my brother. I remember the sterile feel of the place. The cribs seem out of place. The workers all wear white. The floors are shiny. Everything seems surreal. I know that something is terribly wrong with it all. I remember the seemingly large grounds of the hospital. I play and run around large palm trees while mom is inside visiting and comforting my older brother. It is his screams I remember most. I am young, so young I cannot comprehend why my brother is not allowed to come with us. He stands pounding at the sill and side of an open window as we leave. I remember his cries to my mom to come back.

His screams are akin to those of the men who die with me in Vietnam. Many like my brother keep calling out, crying out in voices of such intensity it shatters the air. "Momma, Momma!" Their final hope, their final words are for their mothers. I remember mom shaking and crying as we slowly wave, then turn and leave. In Vietnam, the mothers do not see and feel their son's final tortured moments. Mom sees and feels the anguish, the panic, and bewilderment of my brother.

"Why momma? Why?" I ask over and over again as we make our way down the concrete sidewalk in front of the hospital to the bus stop several blocks away. Mom just shakes and clutches my hand and pulls at me. I turn to look back at the horrible place where they hold my brother. "Why won't they let Billy come with us? Why are they keeping him there?" Tears are streaming down her face. She shakes her head in bewilderment. I cry the tears of a child who cannot comprehend what I take to be utter cruelty, visited upon my brother and mom. I do not cry for myself, but I cry hard, painful, questioning tears. I cannot remember my sister's reaction although she is the strong one in all of this.

• • • •

Grandma Cha 1946

I NEVER KNOW MY DAD'S mom. She dies when he is in high school. Grandma Cha is more than enough. She is for me grand enough for two sets of grandparents. She more than anyone shows me how to act in front of others. Grandma is a star. She can dance, play the Korean drum, act, and most important for Koreans, she can cook. Her Korean food is famous among the small Korean population on O'ahu. "Make us gallons," the Koreans would plead. In the back of her home in Kaimuki I watch her fill big cast iron tubs with chopped cabbages, salt, garlic, chili pepper and water. Heavy stones hold down the brew. After aging outdoors for I know not how long, she transfers the kimchi into gallon jars. Kimchi ages and expands. I see "hot" jugs of kimchi explode their lids off.

· · · ·

The Party

ON A SMALL TABLE IN her kitchen grandma sits me. It could not have been larger than a small desk, but on it she prepares the upcoming feast. As she rushes about, she gives me milk to drink and cookies she has done from scratch. My three-year old eyes follow as she chatters using a mixture of Korean and pidgin English. She sings Korean songs as she chops, kneads, and bakes. This is the prelims for the meal to come. At its heart is the Korean meat. I watch her carefully slice the fatty steak called chuck, cover it, and return it to the refrigerator. As is her custom we retire to her bedroom for her afternoon nap. I hate this part, well the start anyway. My job is to pluck the gray hairs from her head. I feel like a little baboon grooming her. My attention span and patience being an integral part of me, I devise a way of ending my chore. As she dozes off, I wrap several strands of hair around my tiny fist and give it a hard yank! "Aeeeee!" Grandma yells, pops up, then looks down at an apparent sleeping angel. "Chock Say Ah" (you devil) she cries out and pinches my cheek.

The gathering that evening besides our regular clan has several old, single Koreans. Grandma's crude English being what it is requires she give them English nicknames. "Horse Face" is a Korean lady who is long and angular in face and body. "Up and Down" is an old Korean bachelor with a propensity for working the zipper on his trousers while sitting or standing.

Koreans love to laugh and talk in an animated fashion. I do not realize what is getting them so excited. Then the aroma of Korean meat begins to permeate the house. Out back, Grandma squats over a small charcoal hibachi doing her Bul go gee. It is a help yourself affair with adults and children scattered about everywhere.

Just after cleanup while Grandma is in the kitchen they begin chanting. "Hal mu nee" (grandmother) the guests start chanting in unison while clapping and stomping their feet. "Hal mu nee," again and again they ring out as one. My young ears, eyes and sense of cadence blooms. I feel the magic in that sound. They are cheering her on. The person I spent the day watching and playing with is what they want. My grandma.

I watch an actress feign exhaustion at the doorway to the kitchen. "No. No. Too tired," grandma pleads. "Work all day, no, no please." "One dance, Hal mu nee. One dance." "No can."

This brings on chanting again. I first see her eyes get that look, then she raises her hand, and the crowd goes silent. She turns her face dramatically and Bang! Her foot stomps the first beat and off she goes. Beating her drum someone bangs out the beat as grandma waves and twirls to a dance of her native land. I watch her fascinated, seeing how she becomes someone else in an instant.

• • • •

Grandpa Cha

IMPERIAL WINDS BLOW throughout the Pacific. Manifest Destiny infects America's foreign policy. It is our sacred duty to God and our country, the monied elite keep harping. Men with names that would resurface during Ernie's time such as Foster, as in Dulles, and Cabot Lodge hold positions of great influence in the Republican administration of William McKinley. A Republican aristocracy is established that resurfaces during the Eisenhower administration a half century hence.

Just over one hundred years have passed since the English explorer Cook "discovered" the Sandwich Islands. Germany, Spain, England, France, and Holland have established colonies throughout the vast Pacific Basin. Exotic woods, spices, oils, metals, and jewels from these subservient possessions grace the homes and hands of their masters back in Europe. America has been a reluctant participant until the Republican administration of William McKinley. The Democratic administrations have been isolationist. An opportune war with Spain, fanned to fruition by the radical newspaper publisher Hearst, helps propel the formerly reluctant United States into the heady game of imperialism.

With victory over Spain comes the Atlantic possessions of Puerto Rico and a Bay in Cuba, and in the Pacific, the Philippines and Guam. Japan is the only nation in the region to take on the challenge of the European powers and begin its own military dance with destiny.

For grandpa Cha, the year 1903 holds little in the way of historical significance. For him, as with so many of his type, survival is all that matters. Pangs of hunger from deep within his gut distract him. He has neither the time nor inclination to reflect upon things so pedantic as nationalism, grand alliances, kings, presidents, armies, or diplomacy. Grandpa Cha is a commoner. He is one of the masses.

1903 is the year that the white man comes to Korea with an offer he cannot refuse. Work in the cane fields. Sugar needs four things in great abundance to bring it to market. Water, fertile soil, tropical climate, and workers. Hawai'i always has the first three. It is the fourth that proves most elusive. Grandpa Cha is born in 1880 in South Korea. He comes from a family of freaks, as far as the short statured Koreans are concerned. The males of his family stand over six feet in height and the females close to six. But Peter Paul, his Christian given name, is the only normal member of his family at 5'6." Whether this abnormal trait has any bearing will never be known; grandpa Cha's relatives have all died with the exception of one sister by the time he is a young teenager.

An orphan's life is never easy, but it is especially hard in the bleak, cold clime of Korea. The tooth of the Anglo Saxon is indeed sweet. Grandpa Cha comes out of Korea on literally the first boatload of Korean plantation workers. That is how the sugar barons get their cheap field workers. Plague, poverty, and opportunity are what drives successive races of people from their motherlands to Hawai'i.

Grandpa's talents with stone and irrigation soon make him more than a standard field hand. He works on the irrigation canals that flood the fields. Salt preserves foodstuffs. Sugar enhances.

My earliest memories of grandpa Cha are of him sleeping in an alcove at our house in Kailua. He and Grandma don't get along. She has the house at 10th Avenue in Kaimuki. It's a Korean thing. He seems to stand apart from the family. He is wiry and strong. He always looks like an American Indian to me. His eyes are penetrating, his words few.

I watch him while on a weekend outing to Turtle Bay scoop a fish from a small wave that washes onshore one night. I think it is magic. A rare smile and gleam come to his stoic face. He holds it as it snaps in his hand. It is thin and silvery.

• • • •

Extended Family

WE ARE AN EXTENDED family when I am young. We spend almost every weekend together. If we do not go to my grandma Cha's house, the family gathers at mom and dad's. Whenever we could, we would camp together. My earliest recollections are of the times we spend at the various beach campgrounds on O'ahu's northern, southern, leeward, and windward beaches. There are no amenities, no bathrooms or fresh water. The bushes and water we carry in make do. Not many people camp out. I can only recall a few other families who use the beaches for camping. No permits are required. If you find a spot you like, you use it. We would meet at Ewa beach, the North Shore, South Shore near the Blow Hole, and many of the beaches that dot the windward side.

The tribe is made up of my mother's family and the males who have married into the family. I remember grandpa going but not grandma. They do not live together. Grandma has her home where all her children live until they marry. Grandpa lives with us. I do not view this as somehow out of place. It just is the way it is. All the uncles who marry my mother's sisters are white WWII veterans. It seems normal for the family to be bi-racial. It is what I am, and I know nothing else.

Auntie Rose, my mother's younger sister, never marries. She has two children, one from a man who served in WWII, and another from the Korean War. Tripoli is the last name of her son. John is his name, but he is always called Trippi. Rose's daughter Mary uses Spencer, but I remember her father is called Murphy.

Besides mom, who is the oldest, and Rose, there are uncles Sonny, Willie, always called small William, (Daddy is referred to as big William), and the youngest, Mary. Willie is the only single one; he marries after the time we camp. Sonny does not camp with us. He marries a local Chinese woman. Koreans and Chinese do not get along.

• • • •

The Early Years

WE MOVE OFTEN. MOM tells me they owned and lived in over forty homes during their 50 plus years of marriage. My parents increase their equity by playing the favorite capitalist game of Hawai'i. Real estate. We move whenever the value of our home or property escalates to the point where we can step up to a more expensive property.

When we move from Honolulu to Kailua in 1947 it is for investment reasons. Dad now navigates the dangerous Pali Road to his job, across from the Aloha Tower. My young years are a blur of moving and traveling from place to place.

There is a racetrack in Kailua near our house. We'd sneak in and ride some of the horses. I remember being bitten and bucked off on a number of occasions. I remember falling in love with a mysterious blond-haired girl in the first grade. She lives in Kailua for several months before moving back to the mainland. We meet again thirteen years later during a college Easter break. This time we bond for real.

• • • •

Camping 1948

WINDS TASTING OF SALT and seaweed clear the harsh pungent aroma of burlap from my five-year old nostrils. Out through the open flap of our green WWII surplus tent I rush over and across the coarse sanded beach.

I hear them grow in intensity as I make my way. Boom! Boom! Waves unfurl from right to left. Sea to shore, they keep coming unannounced. Deliberately. Tubes of ocean water made translucent from the moonlit night rush up, then quickly pull back into themselves. Cold, salt smelling water foams over and around my chilled bare feet and short thin bare legs.

I stand alone on the bank of hardened sand at water's edge. Swish. Swish. The on-rushing waves, enchanting rhythms of nature kiss me. I stare in innocent wonder across ink-black, vast space and whitecaps that flick on and off under the warm Hawai'i winter's moon. The melodic drumbeat of waves, swirling winds, sea smells calm my restless child's mind.

Earlier that morning I gathered green balls of hard glass from Japan. They are buoys to hold up their fishing nets. Some of the balls of varying sizes have strands of cord still tied to the notched bump made to secure the ball to its net. I find them at the high-water mark. They washed ashore during the previous night's high tide.

"How far is Japan daddy?" I ask.

"Very far," he says as he takes the green ball from my hand and turns it slowly. "See the bubbles in it? They blow these balls by hand. They twist it like this," he says as he mimics the method. "They use a tube. At the end is this," he says, again referring to the ball. "It is made from very hot sand that melts."

"Like this sand, daddy?" I stoop and gather a small boy's handful and show him. He has a smile of recognition that he only shows to me. Daddy is raised in a way that does not show open affection. But the smile he shows leaves no doubt in me that he profoundly loves me.

Daddy seems a brother to me. We are always that way. He is my big brother during such times of learning and exploration. The roles reverse near the end of his life.

We use a large surplus WWII green tent that has a pungent aroma. My dad and uncles spend what seems like a long time putting it up to face the open sea. The tent often buckles and creaks as winds swirl by and over it. We children are placed at the back and sleep on canvas sheeting with woolen blankets that cover us. I'd make an indentation in the sand that holds me like a bird in a nest.

It is an adventure to find wood that we haul back to camp. I remember a fire we make one cold windy night. Driftwood and kiawe (mesquite) that burns red hot is gathered by the men. In a circle of lava rocks a pyre is built. Snaps of cinders fly and break the quiet of the night. There is laughter and muted talk, but mostly we gaze into the flames. The wind keeps shifting and so do I. Hot blasts of heat from the roaring flames strike at me relentlessly.

There are hotdogs and marshmallows which we stick on thin branches. I am not patient. My hotdog burns crinkly and black. My marshmallows all catch fire. I strip their crust and eat the slimy centers of white.

As the fire dies out from lack of fuel, the children are sent to bed. I look back and see their faces. Pensive looks have taken hold. There is a silence. Their faces glow gray. Their clothes are muted and wrinkled.

• • • •

Kahalu'u 1953

I AM NINE WHEN WE JOURNEY from Kailua further into the countryside. We buy a newly offered four-acre lot in Kahalu'u. It is zoned agricultural which fits dad's wish, having a farm. The Hygienic Dairy utilizes most of the valley we live in. There are only four other families on our side of the valley. Our property is hilly and filled with dense undergrowth.

A bulldozer levels off a tier halfway up the hillside. My dad and uncles, all good carpenters, construct a tiny house on the side of the hill. Narrow wooden stairs run up the outside and end on a small porch that looks out over Kahalu'u valley and the Ko'olau mountain range.

There are two tiny bedrooms, one for mom and dad and the other for my brother, cousin John, and me. My sister sleeps in the living room/kitchen area. Downstairs is a bathroom with sink, shower and toilet that empties into a septic tank dug by hand and covered with a wooden top.

We buy a surplus dairy truck and use it to transport building materials for our house, chicken coops, animal pens, and lava rocks that grandpa wants.

Dad builds a tiny pen with sawdust floor under the house. We hand raise peeping chicks and warm them with an overhead light bulb. After a couple of weeks, they move into an above ground hen house at the far end of our terraced area. Grandpa tends them. He builds a small ground pen for ducks.

To this menagerie Dad adds cows, or more precisely young male calves that are now steers. He gets them from the dairy across from us and pays $15 each for them. My brother and I each get one. I name mine Reggie. My brother Bill calls his Jack (aka ass). Dad builds stables for them under the house where the chicks started. We feed them from a bucket with a teat built onto it at the bottom.

Dad gets the milk free. His company is the distributor for Pet Milk in Hawai'i. With the product having to travel by truck, rail, and ship, damages often occur. Flawed or dented cans can- not be sold. These we empty into the bucket and add water. As soon as they wean, we move Reggie and Jack outside to an open pen, down near our neighbor's place.

It is hard work caring for the animals. My brother and I get up at 4:30 AM. It is always dark, oftentimes raining. No boots, barefoot, we trudge out to the pens with buckets of feed for the steers, then back to the shed under the house for a load of grain for the chickens. We wash off in the shower, go upstairs to a hot breakfast, then off to St. Ann's school in Kane'ohe. After school it is the same ritual in reverse, but harder in the heat and sun.

• • • •

Treasures

IT IS AN EARLY SATURDAY morning when my brother and I go to gather grass for our young steers. We take sickles for cutting, rope and burlap for the bundles. Long grasses grow abundantly near the stream below our property.

There are old fruit trees on the abandoned property we walk. Star fruit, mango, and mountain apple trees surround what must have been the back and front yards. There are no signs of a house. For hundreds of years Hawaiians worked this valley. They grew taro and built fishponds where the streams entered the sea.

As I step off the ledge into the thick grass my foot hits it.

"Look at this," I call to my brother. It is a flat, smooth lava rock with carved indentations. It looks like a checkerboard game, called Konane, a game of strategy, won by the person who makes the last move.

"It's too heavy to take back," Billy says. "We have to get this grass cut and packed before it gets too hot." I also find a rounded stone (ulu) made of lava that I leave. This stone was used for Ulu Maika, to see who could roll their stone the farthest down a pre- pared pathway.

We bring back two large bundles of grass. It does not do Reggie or Jack much good. They die soon after. Our neighbor sprays poison all over his place to clear the land to grow papayas. The wind blows enough onto our farm to kill both steers.

We put the bloated Reggie and his brother on a big pile of dry brush and wood scraps, pour gas all over, and light them off into eternity. The smell of rotting flesh roasting on an open fire, mixed with the smoke and ash makes me gag. We slaughter the chickens as a precaution.

My sister is already in high school. She and mom are very close. Betty gets two cute cocker spaniel sisters. They are supposed to be her responsibility. Mom and dad never allow dogs in the house. Dad devises a gate and wire enclosure at the bottom of the stairs to house the dogs at night.

Heat, and I don't mean temperature, brings out the males from throughout the valley. Betty wakes me when she hears them fighting over her babies below. I grab my BB gun, sneak out onto the porch and unload on the bastards. I shoot at their behinds, cause that's what I think of them. But I do not get one of them in time. Ginger (the bitch) gets knocked up, through the wire caging. I check for breaks. None. He must be one skinny little dude.

Daddy and Betty chop off the tails of the litter. Dad shows her how to do stitches. Betty wants to be a doctor someday.

"They're only half cocker spaniel," I say. "They're just mutts. You should leave their tails alone."

"If you hadn't missed, we wouldn't be doing this," dad says, and smiles.

"I know I got three of them," I boast. "I never saw that skinny rat that caused this." It is a lesson about sex, learned on the farm.

My dad is the traffic manager for one of the largest food wholesalers on O'ahu called Fred L. Waldron Company. Prior to the advent of large supermarket chains, wholesalers like the company my dad works for represent the large food and grocery companies.

Hawai'i imports almost every consumer item. Kraft, Kellogg, even Mrs. Smith's bluing, a now defunct firm that made a whitener for clothes, uses my dad's company as their exclusive distributor. Stores can only buy from the wholesalers after the goods are shipped to Hawai'i.

One would not think that race would be an issue in Hawaii. After all, it refers to itself as the "melting pot of the Pacific."

Reality dictates otherwise, however. When my father joins the Kane'ohe Yacht Club, only he and his children can use the facilities; my mother could not. It hurt my mother deeply, but she knows my father's love for sailing and suffers in silence. Despite the prejudice, those young years of mine are happy ones.

The white only restrictions continue to apply until well after Hawai'i attains statehood in 1959, to not only yacht but golf and social clubs as well. Though my dad is highly regarded by the owner of his company, I never remember Mr. Waldron ever so- cializing with my family.

Kane'ohe Bay fronts the large Marine base on the windward side of O'ahu. Living things almost unimaginable in beauty, grace, and color, line the bottom of the protected waters of the Bay.

Color-filled stands of coral, purple, yellow, blue, or red in hue guard the channel from the yacht club out into the bay. On calm days, the water is like a looking glass. Dolphin frolic. A turtle surfaces alongside as we slowly sail by. The shallow bottom reveals a cornucopia of snails, slugs, worms and flashing fish.

One day strong winds snapped at our sail and jib. We struggled as we tacked across the white capped waters. Waves broke over our bow. Suddenly, flying fish shot up out of the sea like darts. They streaked past or struck the sail and jib. Others bounced off the sides of our twelve-foot mini-yacht. One lands inside. Its fins are that of a bird's. Long and bony.

But Hawai'i is growing rapidly in the early 50's. I remember after a good rain the Bay is stained red near its shoreline. Soil from the new subdivisions being built pollute and clog the streams that enter the Bay. Within a few years the once clear wa- ters become a murky brown, no corals or fish to be seen in what had once been a pristine setting. Progress has its price.

There are horses to ride, miles and miles of unspoiled wilderness to explore and unending chores. I imagine myself a Marine when I roam the lush jungle like landscape, BB gun in hand. Little do I know at the time that I am giving myself an invaluable edge that will pay off some twelve years later at a place called Khe Sanh.

I remember one day watching a plane circle our valley. It suddenly does a steep bank to its left, dives, then starts right for me. It is a prop driven dive bomber. The plane is less than fifty feet off the ground. Its big engine roars louder and louder as it zeros in on me.

I fantasize this is the start of another war. I'd be strafed. I duck behind our car. The plane angles off just before reaching me. A guy with a WWII vintage cloth helmet and aviator sunglasses gives me a big shit-eating grin through the plexiglass canopy. As he thunders past my frightened shaking frame, he begins laughing hysterically. He is a Marine from the nearby air station. I flip him off when I regain my composure. I despise Marine

Airedales. They're such arrogant assholes. He answers me by wagging his wings and does a barrel roll while climbing skyward.

Marines are my role models. Kailua and Kane'ohe are towns that off duty Marines from the air station hang out in. They are my scout masters and band instructors. Our cocky styles fit. The Marine Corps is my destiny.

Grandpa Cha has a tiny room built against the outside of the house. He terraces the hillside in front of our house using a pick and shovel. He knows how to pace himself. He swings the pick high above his head then brings it down with a deliberate grunt. He takes several deep lungs full, raises the brown shiny wooden handle and black iron tipped pick and again rips at the firm hard clay. His work is always meticulous. After cutting a small furrow from the hard clay, he takes up a hoe and cuts away the clods of earth. He never leaves a day's work half done. What he does always seems complete.

Grandpa carries the rocks from their large pile at the base of our property and lays them in level neat piles by our winding driveway that stretches from the end of the cul-de-sac to the top. He carves a shallow trench, stakes small pieces of wood, and joins them with white cord. His level is of tarnished wood with three bubbles at different angles. His patience in this process amazes me.

He spends what seems to me hours in preparation measuring, judging, eyeing closely and from a distance his planned wall. All I see is a shallow trench, bordered by string and sticks. He turns the porous black stones that spewed from the ground cen- turies earlier in his hands, examining them like a surgeon would before the cut is made.

He uses a small mallet whose handle of wood is shiny from his old hand. The end is of squared black iron. He gently taps at the stone until a small section breaks away. He turns the rock, examines, then taps again and again, until the piece is perfect.

He makes of his work an elaborate jigsaw puzzle. Stone upon stone he builds the wall from the base of the hill to halfway up the driveway. He uses cement that he mixes in a bucket to bond the layers of rock. He tops the wall with a very thin layer and lets it set. It takes him months.

Sixty years later I run my hand over the knee-high wall that meanders only a hundred feet. I have grown and aged. The wall has shrunk in my minds-eye. The once white top now bears the wear of years and is almost the color of the earth. Not a split or crack can be seen. The owners of the property speak in amazement of the strength and durability of grandpa's wall.

"We hit it with trucks and machinery when we redid the land to make it into a nursery," the man says. "We always wondered who had made such a strong, beautiful wall."

"It is something special," his wife concurs with a nodding of her smiling face.

I love those years I spend in Kahalu'u. I attend St. Ann's grammar school in nearby Kane'ohe. My mom takes us in her car. There is no bus service. Some kids even ride their horses to school.

Ranch lands surround the school. Kids swim in nearby streams on hot days after school. It is without question the best years of my life.

• • • •

First Transition 1954

I'M IN FOURTH GRADE. I see Uncle Willie with the principal walk into my class. Four days earlier I watched grandpa coughing up blood in his room. He had lost weight rapidly. I get daddy and daddy carries grandpa in his arms down the hill to the car. There is no 911. Daddy drives over the old Pali Road to Saint Francis Hospital in Honolulu.

"Your grandfather died," Uncle Willie says softly to me. "He had leukemia. Your mom and dad have arrangements to make. I'm taking you to stay with family friends."

My teacher makes the sign of the cross and touches my shoulder.

"We will pray for your family, Ernest," she says. Her kind old face is framed in white and black. Her costume is a habit. She has a ring on her right finger and says she's a bride of Christ. I doubt her. I am not twelve and already an Agnostic. I leave with Uncle Willie filled with remorse for not bonding with grandpa like I have with grandma.

I'm beginning to see myself as a part of, rather than a singular being. Grandpa's wake, rosary, and Catholic burial are bewildering, frightening, and mystical.

I never see my grandparents speak to one another. Grandma makes up for it once grandpa can't talk back.

At his wake, my grandmother plays the part of the bereaved wife to the hilt. Koreans wail operatically. When the doors are opened for the family to enter the visitation room, grandma "bum-rushes" his open casket.

"Ayeee! No, No," she screams out while dramatically moving to him. Her all-white Korean mourning dress trails behind her. At the coffin she wails, claws at her hair, begging God to take her and not him. She hated him. Grandpa didn't give a shit what she thought. She would not look at him whenever they shared living space. The magic of death has cured her negative feelings for him.

Dressed in white, the Korean sign of mourning, I sit with my family on chairs facing grandpa's still being. People pass slowly by, shaking my hand and mumbling words I never hear. I am in shock and at awe with it all. From the banquet room next to us, Koreans roar with animated laughter while feasting on mounds of food.

I think nothing can top the wake, but at the gravesite the next day grandma proves me wrong. She is somber and silent while sitting on her chair facing the coffin, but as soon as the priest finishes his gig and the undertakers begin lowering the cof- fin, grandma springs out of her widow's chair.

"Wait, wait for me," she yells, begging. My two uncles know better and get up behind her. As they grasp her, she struggles against them trying to leap into the grave. Then, proving her point, she falls back into their arms in a dramatic swoon.

Grandma is always the star at every family gathering. Her bullshit is always so creative, artistic, and over the top. It is all I can do not to laugh out loud.

Mom notices me smirking. She gives me her nasty look. Her lips whispering "stop." I leave the crowd at the graveside. Walking to the car I notice Diamond Head rising above my left shoulder. Grandpa and Grandma will lie for all eternity in the shadow of this ancient volcano, Hawai'i's symbol of Aloha.

• • • •

Light 1954

FROM THE OPEN PORCH of our house perched against the hillside I stand one morning gripping the flimsy railing made of 2x4s. To my right a small squall is blowing across

Kane'ohe Bay. It is headed right at me. Rain falls in curtains of white from the dark gray underbelly of the cloud mass. I see and feel it move slowly by. It's boiling, churning inside. I can smell it.

It misses me by 200 yards. Our neighbor's place on the hill across from me is showered. In but a minute sunlight pushes the cloud onward toward the Ko'olau cliffs. As it nears the mountain, rainbows of vibrant colors arch to life from its sides, then fade as the black mass spreads over the mountainside. Slowly, the black mass rises while raining down on the re-emerging mountain. Giant waterfalls spew white over verdant green sides of the ridges. The mountain is not shear but etched with endless thin valleys that look like jagged scars Pele left in her haste to finish O'ahu and move on to Molokai.

Mists abound. The mountain is a canvas for the sun. Colors of green, blue and mist white swirl. Shadows and light define the crags and valleys in front of me.

As the wet fades, colors change from yellowish green to light blue to emerald, changing as the sunlight bounces off and dances through the wetness.

I gasp at the utter beauty. I look about. There is no one to be seen. I am alone, and enchanted.

• • • •

Laie 1955

OUR EXTENDED FAMILY spends most weekends together. Our house at Kahalu'u is too small. When beachfront lots at Laie go up for sale, mom and dad buy one for $15,000. The lot is a sand dune that slopes gently to the water. Dad and my uncles build a rectangular shack facing the ocean.

• • • •

Torching

A REEF STARTS NEAR water's edge and extends a quarter of a mile out. We can walk on it at low tide. My brother and I with four adults gather at water's edge at low tide. It's the dark night of a new moon. We hold two kerosene lanterns and a torch fashioned from a gallon can nailed onto the end of a round pole. It is stuffed with rolled burlap. Kerosene is added. Daddy uses a match. A bright orange flames to life. "Let's go," daddy orders. We carefully step over the flat coral shelf that is pocked with small pools of water. The bottoms of my feet are so tough I hunt barefoot. It is in these shallow pools we find them. Until the tide rises again, they are trapped. I carry a short, two-pronged spear. We are a feral pack hunting whatever moves or swims.

• • • •

Selling Out

WE ARE IN THE LIVING room of our cramped, small home. Betty and my brother are seated on her bed near the window. I am standing beside our front door. Dad and mom telling me why we are moving once again.

"Your sister is starting college. Your brother needs a good school. We found a beautiful big house in Manoa," mom says. "All of you can take the bus to school. Your father will not have that long trip to work anymore."

"But what about me, mom? What about me? Don't I count?" The snot from my crying is dripping down my lip and the side of my face. "I like being here and Laie, at the beach. I ride horses. I go fishing. I don't care about school."

"Ern," daddy says softly. "You'll love Manoa, I promise."

I yank open the screen door and storm out. I'm at the corner of our rickety porch, hands on the railing, looking out at my sacred Ko'olau mountains. I hear the screen door open, then quietly shut. I turn and see mom.

"May I please talk to you, my son?" I nod and turn back to my mountain. "I've never told you this before, my son, but I was not supposed to even have you." I am now the priest in the con- fessional.

"The first time I took your brother to see Doctor Gaspar, he looks at me real angry and says, 'If you have another one, you'll both die.'" She begins crying. "But I knew I had to have you, my son. I knew in my heart I had to have you," she repeats, choking back tears. "You are my dream, my son. There is nothing you can't do if you set your mind to it."

I am alone once again on the porch gazing out at my enchanted valley and special friend, the mountain. Mom does not convince me. Education always comes first for mom. Bill and I will go to Maryknoll because that's what she wants.

She went to Maryknoll on a full scholarship; she works in the library to "earn" her tuition. In her junior year, the nuns tell her she will get a full scholarship to Catholic University in Washington, D. C. when she graduates. The sisters of Maryknoll have two full scholarships a year to give out to promising girls from the Hawaiian Islands.

Grandma makes her quit later that year because she finds mom a job. The Depression is raging. Mom becomes a maid on Ford Island in Pearl Harbor, working for a first lieutenant and his family. That lieutenant can afford two servants.

My dad is in the Army with the air division (they had planes on Ford Island). It is a typical Hawai'i love story. Local girl falls in love with a soldier from the mainland.

. . . .

Move to Leeward Side

WE MOVE TO THE LEEWARD side of O'ahu when I enter the seventh grade. My sister is entering the University of Hawaii and there is no Catholic high school on the windward side of the Island for my brother to attend. We settle in Manoa valley, near the University of Hawai'i. Maryknoll, the Catholic grade and high school that my brother and I attend, is also close by.

• • • •

O'AHU AVENUE 1956

My parents' master bedroom and bath take up the entire back of the mansion. Their bedroom and bath are larger than our houses in Kahalu'u and Laie combined. My sister has her own bedroom. She shares a full bathroom with my brother and me. Our bedroom is at the front of the house, next to a huge living room. Billy and I have our own walk-in closet. We never use the maid's unit that's built beside the garage. Our home is on the wide boulevard in Manoa called O'ahu Avenue. There is a stoplight and bus stop at the intersection three homes down from us.

• • • •

Korean Gangsters

IT'S SUMMER. WE ARE still unpacking. I'm sitting on the curb in front of our house, scoping out what's around me. I'm amazed at everything. The curb is made of carved black stones, cemented at each joint. The wide avenue has new striping that trails off to my right like a snake.

I see a guy my age walking to me from two houses away. He is wearing khaki Bermuda shorts and has a big smile with a front tooth rimmed in gold.

"I'm Henry Kim," he says, looking down on me. "What school are you going to?"

"Maryknoll," I answer and stand. "Hmpf," he sniffs. "I go to Punahou."

"You don't look like a haole (white)," I sneer. He laughs out loud.

"Naw. We got a few Koreans at Punahou. See that house over there?" He points at the two-story white house across from us at the corner. "Kerry lives there. He goes to Punahou, too. Both his parents are Korean. Me? I'm half. My mom's part Hawaiian. How about you?"

"My dad's haole. Mom is full Korean," I say. His face goes full on.

"No shit? Wow! We can make our own Korean gang."

Kerry is the most stable of the three of us. From Kerry's attic window we shoot firecracker balls with slingshots at the cars when they stop for red lights. Slingshots were a compromise. Henry wants us to use BB guns. Loaded guns are not allowed in Kerry's home. Henry has a 22 rifle and shoots at Mynah birds from his porch when his parents are at work.

Henry goes to The Naval Academy after graduating from Punahou. He flies carrier jets and dies flying a forest fire spotter plane after retiring from the Navy. Kerry goes to Tuskegee Institute, the black university, and becomes a veterinarian.

· · · ·

The Opposite Sex, Manoa 1957

THE FIRST TIME I KISS a girl is in first grade, Kailua 1949. Actually, she kisses me. I'm playing with my friend Smally when she sneaks up and pecks me on my cheek. I turn, looking into her blue eyes. A smile embraces me. Her honey blond hair flies behind her as she runs away from me. She's beautiful, and like Smally, her dad is a Marine at Kaneohe Marine Corps Air Base.

Today Henry tells me there's a Punahou girl who has the hots for me. She lives in the Manoa Triangle area.

"Her folks are out for the night," he says, a leer in his look. "She's hot, Ernie." I'm barefoot in my best pair of jeans and a T-shirt. Henry is wearing Bermuda shorts, penny loafers without socks and a shirt with a collar.

"Wait here," he says and goes into the house. After a minute Henry opens the front door and ushers me in. He leads me to a back bedroom. "I'll wait in the living room," he says.

It is her bedroom. She's reclining on a girl's bed, dressed in white short shorts and a blouse that shows the crease of her small breasts. Her initial smile of anticipation turns critical as she sizes me up. She looks me over like I'm a model on a runway.

"You look like a country boy," she says in a mocking way.

"What'd you just say?" My eyes go full pissed off. I feel my teeth clench. She laughs. I turn and walk to the door.

"Hey, I was just playing with you, Ernie. Don't go."

"You're not my type," I say slamming her door behind me. Henry sees me coming at him.

"What happened?" Henry grabs my arm. I pull away.

"Fuck Punahou, Henry." I walk home alone. I'm not going out with any Punahou girls.

• • • •

The Courtyard 1957

IT IS WHERE WE ASSEMBLE in the mornings before class. David plays the bugle. We stand at attention. Then, after honoring America we march up wooden stairs to rooms that hold 50 plus students from K through 8. The courtyard is paved. It is for lunch, play and even carnivals.

Maryknoll girls are more my type. I want to kiss all of them. Lunch and recess are like a Hawaiian version of the Spanish Paseo. I'm shooting a basketball at the hoop, but my eyes are following them.

• • • •

Me Too 1957

I HAD GOTTEN A HEADS up several days earlier.

"He went try get in my pants, Ernie," Peter says. Peter and I are both altar boys. I watch as the pathetic old priest shuffles into our class. He heads directly for the nun at the front.

"Ernest," Sister calls out proudly, "Father wants to talk to you." The naïve woman thinks I'm going to heaven. She is absolutely delighted that the priest wants me. I glance over at Peter. He is wide eyed and frightened for me.

I walk out with my chin up knowing what's coming. This stupid pervert is not getting me. I've always done well under stress. I come alive in an invigorating way. Fear. It is fear that gives me the adrenaline rush.

I ignore him as he tries to make idle chatter on the way to his residence. The housekeeper is not there. He leads me up the stairs to his private office. It is small. A desk faces the door, a chair in front of the desk.

"Sit down," he says, as he takes his. I feel like the character Al Pacino in the movie The Godfather where he's getting ready to shoot Sterling Haydon, the corrupt police captain. I don't hear any of the bullshit the priest is mouthing until he says the magic words: "Do you know about sex?"

"Yeah." My answer is short and harsh. I really see him now.

"Noo," he says jumping to his feet. "Let me show you!" He scurries around his desk. He's shaking, especially his hands. I stand, like a man, and push my chair back. His eyes are on my crotch. He walks blindly into my right fist and goes down hard.

"Oooo," I hear him moaning as I slam his door and fly down the stairs. I'm pumped walking across the courtyard back to class. What if I really hurt him?

I didn't, and when my mom asks why I am quitting the altar boys I say:

"It's not for me.

. . . .

Saint Louis Heights 1957

"ERNIE," SHE SAYS, KISSY face, hand out, asking me to dance. It is the garage of her place. Open, it gives great night views of Waikiki and Honolulu. Crepe paper stringers decorate. Fruit punch is sipped from paper cups. Our eighth-grade class is dancing to Rock and Roll. Well, the girls anyway. Most of the boys are shy and don't dance. I do.

It's a slow one now. I hold her tight. I can feel all of her pressing into me. She pulls her face away from mine and kisses me with an open mouth like a woman. It leaves me breathless.

. . . .

Rite of Passage 1957-1958

WHO COULD BLAME AMERICANS for feeling good about themselves? 1957 is a good time to be middle class in America. Humbled Germans and Japanese can only stare and marvel, as Yankee know-how cranks out classic after classic, persons and things, from Chevy to Elvis. It is the age of enlightenment in advertising. If it is glitzy, glamorous, and new, it is American.

America is a place where one working male could easily support a wife, kids, dog, house, and car. The good life is affordable. People who had known depression as children, war and sacrifice as young adults, now are feeding on the good life. They don't lock their doors. They are not afraid. More than anything, they trust their institutions, government, leaders, and stars.

On warm fall Friday evenings across America, TVs blink in unison through open windows. Adult laughter from unafraid homes light up the darkness of otherwise quiet neighborhoods.

Nearby at dark drive-in theaters, movies play for their inat- tentive children. In front and back of big-seated automobiles blemish-faced teens neck and grope with emerging glandular urges of the most powerful sort. Junior's nuts burn and start to turn blue.

"Don't," she'd say as he tries once more to navigate simultaneously under her shirt and bra. Gas is a quarter, burgers twelve cents. Unless you are poor, you can afford a good time. Radio and TV are free. Advertising takes care of that.

Ike's lame duck attitude seems more inclined towards golf than world affairs or domestic issues. A young TV prophet named Reagan goes unrecognized as he accurately foretells the future for himself and General Electric.

Communism is America's boogey man. It fits the needs of corporate interest groups and organized religion. Both General Electric and the Roman Catholic Church champion the call for decisive action against godless Communism.

Ike departs the scene with a prophetic warning about the military industrial complex, but Americans are not listening. Those manning the factories and offices have bitter memories of depression and two wars. With General Electric showing the way they can have it all, appliances, protection, and good paying jobs. GE gives the impression that it is primarily electric, but its profits come from nuclear, as in submarines and missiles.

• • • •

Maryknoll

IN MANOA THE BUSES stop three houses down from us. My sister uses one bus line to the University of Hawai'i while Billy and I ride the other to Maryknoll.

Strange things happen spontaneously during adolescence. Erections, emotions, life is surreal for the budding teenager. Uniforms help blind both nuns and students as to what is really going on.

In my freshman year I am introduced to the military lifestyle. JROTC. Junior Reserve Officer's Training Corps. Every Monday we play dress up. In starched tan khaki trousers with matching long sleeved shirts and tie we prance and parade. All males in high school in Hawai'i are required to take JROTC. Two years if you are in a public school and four in most of the private high schools. I hope someday to be a real soldier.

Beneath a broiling tropical sky, hup, two, three, four, march khaki clad mixtures of ethnic races with exotic looks. In rows and columns, they march to barked commands from instructors paid for by the Defense Department. Professors of Military Science and Tactics they are called. Even tiny Maryknoll has two.

So much is revealed about a culture when one examines its rituals. Acts of sadistic cruelty are frequently performed on young males during rites of passage. Permanent marking is often used, such as tattoos, teeth filing or penis trimming.

The Catholic method utilizes pomp and ceremony. The gaudier and more pretentious the uniforms so much the better. Maryknoll outdoes the other Catholic schools; it makes ROTC mandatory all four years instead of the state mandated two.

Maryknoll is a missionary order of Catholic black robes. There is a historical correlation, a trail if you will, of Catholic conquest that often follows successful military incursions. Hawai'i bristles with military installations. Soldiers, sailors, marines, and airmen stroll predictable sections of town or nestle in bars geared to their peculiar fantasies. The wants and needs of the soldier are timeless. Alcohol and prostitutes consume their pay.

Those smiling innocent virgins from New England who teach as nuns at Maryknoll never acknowledge the darker side of military life. Drill team is a varsity sport as prized as basketball at Maryknoll.

Nuns love order and discipline. Prayer, cold showers, and stiff, starched uniforms help combat their own feminine agenda. "No talking," a stern nun would hiss, her face flush from unex- pressed sexuality. Maryknoll is a concept based more in fantasy than reality.

The Catholic Church has a soft spot in its heart for converting and maintaining as converts...Pagans. A sinister sounding word if ever there was one. Righteous feeling, unrestrained breeding, middle class working people of New England give in abundance for their missions. From their collection baskets pours the nectar of mother Church. Cash. Prohibition against artificial means of birth control produces a bountiful harvest for the Church. Sunday Masses on the hour can barely accommodate the fertile families. One breeding couple and brood can take up an entire pew or more. Priests sweat through Mass after Mass. Overseas, missions build schools.

My naive young teachers come from large New England families. Why would one leave one's home for a life in some hot, sweaty mission? Can it be they are mind fucked? Are these innocent young girls confused by religious ritual, dogma and promises that fly in the face of their reality at home? What about the dark side of their families' lives? One often hears the nun extol her "saintly" mother, but not dad. Did the secret of the "bottle" rule dad's life?

New England Catholic homes are often crowded, noisy and stressful. Twelve people live in a small house with one bathroom. Chastity and wedded bliss to the Son of God Almighty might well appear attractive in such circumstances.

My fantasies collide head on and merge with the dreams and fantasies of these young, New England virgins. If they have to dress in hot, long black robes, and wear head coverings like TV screens and walk to jangling rosaries on black witches' shoes then the little heathens could, too. Nuns cannot play house to their inner urges, but they can play make believe with violence. The wives of Jesus grin and nod in blissful glee as I and my rifle-shouldered male classmates march in step while passing in review.

The nuns have not a clue what they are doing. They can't possibly foresee the consequences of their labor. Within a short decade's time those young men they help indoctrinate will perish in body and soul in Vietnam.

Those boys become bit players in the Church's grander scheme and plans, a donation if you will, to fight Communism. The cause is just, the need urgent, so the Vatican claims. A uniform to match a young man's dreams, they give those young native knights. Sally forth, young lads, to slay the dragon and save the princess.

In stiff brown khaki shirt, pants and synchronized shiny black shoes, they pass again in review. Sunlight glistens off their polished brass buttons, belts, and epaulets. We are children, playing make believe.

. . . .

Hot Shot Maryknoll High School 1958

I AM THE PERSON I WANT to be. I love this school. I'm just a freshman. I'm the best shot on the rifle team. I'm popular with my peers. The nuns are progressive. One old one smiles like a proud mother whenever she sees me. They encourage us to socialize. We have school sponsored military balls with music and dancing. A lei gets you a kiss. It's an old Hawaiian custom.

I'm at the front door of her house. I'm dressed in my uniform, corporal stripes on my sleeves.

"Oh, hi Ernie," she says after opening the front door. She's got crinolines on that make her look like we're in the movie Gone with the Wind. She steps onto the porch. She's looking right into

my eyes and me. As I place a red carnation lei around her neck she giggles. I put my lips onto hers, softly, while tilting my head to fit her mouth. What a way to start!

A cool passing trade wind blows gently by the warm evening outside the ballroom in Waikiki. We are giddy as we stroll holding hands that swing in time. Sacred orange torches guide our way along a romantic stone path, greened with plants of the tropics.

We kiss again and embrace one another with lips and arms that tremble with exploding passion. Everything smells, seems, and feels new when you're that young, and just that old. Her lovely young neck is rimmed with carnations of red. Her crinolines bounce beneath a flared skirt. She smiles that womanly smile known to melt men's hearts and does mine. Could this be love, this young make-believe soldier wonders? No———it is just a rite of passage.

And ten years later will come another, where I sit hunched over, feeling all alone and shake in fear, the thick padding of my flak jacket pressing against my neck with each jerk. Life shakes, as rockets whistle, roar, and bang their reminders of war's reality. "Dance with this," the angry goddess of war hisses in my ear.

What boy of fourteen sees future consequences in innocent endeavors? I am on the varsity rifle team as a freshman. I am a hot shot, who shoots tiny targets 50 feet away, not men. The role of soldier gets me what all people crave and need. Respect.

Had I been Hawaiian and lived twenty years later and gone to Kamehameha school, I might have gone in for hula instead. But hula is not the ticket now. I play the games given me. I win a trophy that says I am the Freshman of The Year. The nuns beam, some boys sneer, and the girls smile with kissy faces.

At a party for my departing, tears stream down the face of my latest flame.

"I'll write you," she promises. Only emptiness I feel, for I am moving to LA.

Family needs and not my desires, decide. The educational needs of my sister and brother cannot be met in Hawai'i. And it would take more money than the Spencer's have to send them away to school.

This has all been gently explained to me by my parents, but I cannot feel good about this move. Not at all. My heart speaks loud and clear. LA is a mistake. As I dance a last time and kiss her goodbye I feel no passion from the kiss, nor her body held snug against me, only profound dread.

I do not want to move to the mainland. I love my school, my friends, and my lifestyle in Hawai'i.

• • • •

Mauna Loa 1958

WE ARE ON A HUNTING trip to the Big Island. A professional guide drives daddy, Billy, John and me from Hilo up the mountain in his Jeep. We are near the top of the mountain. Feral, wild sheep flush from a lava flow in front of us.

I carry a rifle from World War II daddy bought for $19. It's the same model rifle that kills President Kennedy five years later. Mine doesn't have a telescope like Lee uses on JFK.

I focus on a large ram in the middle of five ewes. Explosions of lava mark our shots that miss. Daddy and Billy empty their rifles and quit. I reload. They are now 400 yards away and going uphill. I drop the ram on my third shot. Daddy has a wide ass grin on his face.

"Nice shot, Ern," Billy says.

On the Road Again June 1958

I'm so pissed off I don't speak to my parents for several days. My brother has been accepted to Loyola University in Los Angeles. Daddy believes Billy will make a great engineer. Betty is going to Cal State Northridge to become a teacher. I'm going to an all-boys Catholic high school in the heart of L.A. called Mount Carmel. It's closed now and is a children's playground.

. . . .

High School 1958-1961

WE MOVE TO LOS ANGELES in the fall of 1958 after my freshman year of high school. Mom's dream is that all her children receive the college education she was denied by her mother. Dad is a risk taker. He feels he can earn more money on the mainland than in Hawai'i.

. . . .

Mount Carmel High School

MY THREE YEARS IN LOS Angeles are the worst in my life. It is worse than Vietnam. I chose the Marines, but not LA.

My eyes are tearing, I'm coughing, choking on the smog as dad drives us. We can fill our tank with leaded gasoline for a couple of bucks. We get 8 miles a gallon on a crowded freeway and arteries that lace this heartless city. No seat belts mean ugly deaths. Weekends on the Hollywood Freeway are good for at least one or two lives cut short, but for a simple safety device.

I hate living in Los Angeles. I despise my school, Mount Carmel. It took up an entire city block at 70th and Hoover Street. Just up the street is the University of Southern California. The neighborhood is gentrifying.

Around the outside of the fenced campus Pachucos strut on the cement sidewalks. We are told to only leave campus in groups. The Mexican boys with their slicked back hair, funny pants, and switchblade knives are to be avoided. They like to fight. They bait the white boys from outside the fence, whistling and kissing at them. Respect is earned.

Each grade has two classes of about fifty students. Those three years are hard on me. I do not fit in. I feel like an outsider. I become known as "the pugilist." A friendly priest who teaches English and Latin gives me that nickname. Fighting is fashionable. It is a masculine thing. Boys might not like you, but they do respect you when you kick their ass. The white guys are afraid of me. The black, Asian and Hispanics respect me.

The guys form a large circle and cheer and jeer as I knock the shit out of guys who push me too far. I am subjected to racial taunts. I knock guys out with my overhand right cross after pop- ping their heads back with my strong left jabs. I take naturally to fighting. It does not frighten me. There is an intensity to it that brings out the animal in me.

• • • •

Brother Lawrence

IT IS LUNCHTIME ON the asphalt commons. A large crowd encircles me. The guy in front of me is covered in blood. I've dropped him twice and let him get back up. The few black students are screaming at me to stomp him.

He's the guy nobody messes with because his dad is in the mob. The "word" is that his dad owns a trucking company that's a front for the Italian mafia in L.A. The actor Lou Costello hangs out with the priests here, so who knows?

This bloody, big nosed punk has a high duck ass hairstyle that's now plastered to his face, dripping blood. I've broken his nose. His lower lip is fat and cracked. I feel a hand come down on my right shoulder. I turn and see the tall Brother Lawrence looking down at me.

"Enough," he says. "Go wash your face," he tells my oppo- nent. He motions me with his chin to follow him.

Brother Lawrence is the school disciplinarian. It is a fulltime job keeping a school filled with horny, testosterone filled males in line.

"Sit down," he says motioning me to a chair in front of his desk. From his desk drawer he takes a pack of Pall Mall unfiltered cigarettes, lights one and tosses me the pack and lighter. I fire one up and exhale. "You whopped him real good, Ernest," he says. "It's good for the school that you did it." He takes another drag and blows upward. "I'll talk to his dad. I'll tell him his boy lost a fair fight." I stand to leave. He says, "Leave the cigarette. You know there's no smoking on campus." He has a big proud smile on his face.

"Thanks for the smoke, Brother," I say crushing it out in the glass ashtray.

• • • •

The Nazi's Son 1959

HE COMES UP TO ME IN the hallway shortly after I kick the Italian's ass. He's fair, almost albino. His hair is thin and ultra-blonde.

"I would like to socialize with you," he says, extending his small hand. "I am Petshaur, from Germany." His words are sharp. They slice through the air. He looks like a stereotypical little Nazi I see in movies.

I'm now riding next to him in his two-seater coupe.

"So, what does your dad do for a living?" My idle question gets a quick response.

"He works for the government. It's secret." His round, thick gold rimmed glasses frame a sweating red face. He looks over at me and repeats, "My father works for the US government. He is a top-secret man."

The Petshaurs live in a small, nondescript home near the Skunk Works. There is a small German community of scientists in Los Angeles. A number of their children attend Mount Carmel.

"Where's your mom?" I ask as soon as I enter the home. It is sparse, bare.

"There is only me and my father," he says.

The living room and dining area are one. Cold faded wallpaper and sparse, hard furnishings capture my eyes.

Next to a cheap four seat dining table, on the wall is a single mounted black and white photo. Drawing me to it, he points.

"That is my father." He is a tall thin man standing at attention in a Nazi uniform with SS lightning bolts on his collar. "He was a very high rank officer," Petshaur says proudly.

Petshaur disappears near the end of sophomore year. I hope the Jews got him.

• • • •

The Four Amigos 1960

MOUNT CARMEL GUYS LIVE segregated lives. Race, place, and finances determine the social order. Even the football players leave after the games alone or in small packs. At lunchtime socializing takes place out in the cars. Guys eat baloney sandwiches, smoke cigarettes, and listen to rock and roll on the radio.

Mike, Tom, Jim, and I begin hanging together just before summer. Jim's dad is a carpenter who spends the week up north at Vandenberg. The government is building a new missile base. His dad also brews his own beer and stores it in the garage. Screw cap quart bottles with labels like Miller, Budweiser, and Schlitz line the back wall.

"Help yourself," Jim says. The fluid is light green and flaked with what looks like small coconut chips. "It will get you off, I promise," Jim says with a big ass grin.

Tom's car is a two-door coupe with seats for two. Behind the seats two can squat, but since Mike and I smoke, we get relegated to the trunk. The combination of having to lie on our back, a bumpy ride to the beach, and smoking without ventilation cause both Mike and me to get roaring drunk after one quart each. "Holy shit!" Tom yells when he opens the trunk. The smoke pours out. Jim is laughing. "Hey, I'll get a towel and do smoke signals."

I fall out of the trunk onto my face. Mike steps out onto me and goes down. We are both laughing hysterically.

It is an hour later. Mike and I are almost sober. We're tossing a football. A group of rich kids in fancy beach clothes walk by.

"Huh," a skinny guy who is prancing says, "I didn't know they allowed Japs on this beach." I spring at him like a cat. "Eeeee!" he screams, raising his hands to his face.

I crack him with an open right hand across the side of his face. I take him by his throat. "I'm not a Jap you little queer."

"I'm sorry, I'm sorry," he's begging me. I push him away.

"Get the fuck off my beach."

• • • •

Busted 1960

MY SISTER IS LIVING away from home. I have been out with friends. Dad's car is home. He should be at the liquor store. When I walk in the door my brother is sobbing in the living room. Dad is there with mom. "I'm throwing your father out," mom says to me. "He's been having an affair with a damn German," she says with a vile sneer. "Her husband came and told me. And I have this," she says waving a small black book. "There's over 300 names in it. He kept a record of all his conquests."

My life becomes real all of a sudden. Dad says nothing. He looks down, ashamed.

"You'll go with your brother and me," mom says. "I'm staying with dad," I say quickly. Mom's face contorts into a strange painful silent cry. She gasps. Her eyes slant even more.

"Come here," she says to dad. They disappear into their bedroom. My brother and I sit quietly, thinking our own thoughts. An hour later Dad comes out and leaves.

"We're going to work it out," Mom comes out and tells us.

I go out into our backyard and sit beside the pool. Over the fence, on the busy street, I hear car tires slicing through the dark night.

• • • •

Stake Out 1961

WHEN WE LEAVE HAWAI'I dad buys a liquor store on Western Avenue in Los Angeles. The Cuban who sells it helps dad build a brand new one on a vacant lot next door. It is big with a neon sign and has a glass front. Armed robbery is a problem in Los Angeles. Liquor stores are a favorite, especially late at night. Dad was a reserve cop in Hawai'i, and he befriends the L.A. police. They often stop by to have a soda and chat. Dad is a man's man and loves joking around with them. I work part time as a stock boy. I fill the walk-in refrigerator and restock the shelves.

I'm looking up at the cop in street clothes. He's sitting on a stool on top of the walk-in refrigerator and cradling an M1 car- bine with a 30-round clip. He's hidden behind boxes smoking a cigarette and looking bored.

Dad tells me to stay in back if any males walk in, especially black men. Blacks are robbing liquor stores at night throughout our section of Los Angeles.

I never take or drink liquor from my dad's store. I go to Watts where the blacks live and buy mine. We'd give a guy hanging out in front of a liquor store a couple of dollars to buy us a couple of six packs of beer. The black dudes are always funny and accommodating.

"You boys don't do nothen I wouldn't. You understand what I'm sayen?" The old dark wino gives us a wink and bids us goodnight. He gets a half pint of whiskey and tall can of beer to chase it with the money we give him.

I hate it here. I feel so out of place. Los Angeles has no soul, or customs of its own, only endless blocks of tacky houses or single- story stores selling almost anything but happiness.

· · · ·

I'm a Full-Grown Ass Man 1961

IN MY SENIOR YEAR OF high school, I am offered a chance to attend Gonzaga University in Spokane Washington, Saint Mary's in Orinda California, and Chaminade College (now University) in Honolulu.

I turn 18 in May. I am determined to get away from this miserable place. Dad has other ideas. He knows what occupations his children would do best. Betty is an educator. Billy will be an engineer and I will be an attorney. That's what my folks think. Well, they get two out of three.

I pick Saint Mary's in Moraga near San Francisco. But just before we graduate, Chaminade College in Honolulu sends a recruiter to Los Angeles. The Marianists have a high school here. When I find out Chaminade has a dorm, I sign up. Mom just rolls her eyes when I tell them.

"I wish you'd stay, Ern," dad says sadly as he drives me to the airport.

"I'm going home, dad. That's what I want."

. . . .

Chaminade 1961-1965

CHAMINADE IS BUILT at the base of a narrow ridgeline that slants down the western side of the Ko'olau mountain range. O'ahu and the other islands of the chain once called the Sandwich Islands are split in two by a single, tall dominating range of volcanic made mountain. The mountains formed islands windward side up and leeward down on the map. Most rains come from the north and east. The windward sides are wetter and greener than the leeward sides.

Honolulu is on the leeward, eastern side of O'ahu, the most populated island in the chain of six inhabited islands. Chaminade overlooks the section of Honolulu called Kaimuki. From Saint Louis Heights, Chaminade looks down at Waikiki and over onto Diamond Head.

The Marianist missionaries came to Hawai'i in the late eighteen-hundreds as teachers. They establish schools on O'ahu, Maui, and the Island of Hawai'i. They teach only boys. Saint Louis High next to my college is the original school. In the late nineteen fifties the Marianists start Chaminade and build a seminary there for their priests and brothers in training.

My dormitory stands precariously on the hillside at the south end of the property. They were poorly constructed sitting atop rickety thin wooden legs and adorned with roofs topped with a thin layer of tarpaper.

Less than twenty years has passed since the chatter of nurses filled these hastily erected dorms. The school was used during WWII as a hospital. Wounded from the Pacific Theater flowed back to the safety of the Hawaiian Islands. Some were treated on these grounds.

When I attend Chaminade there are less than 500 students. One, two-story building with a basement houses the student body. From the outside second floor balcony that gives access to the classrooms you can look out at Waikiki just a couple of miles away.

The dormitory that houses the seminarians is the first new construction since the building of the two original, two story units that are used for teaching.

I walk up the ramp into the lower dorm that houses the freshman students. The upper dorm is used by several priests and upper classmen.

Constant rain has been with us for several days. We are restless in our cramped quarters. The winded raindrops - angled against our teetering, termite infested dorm - levels out into a constant patter. It seems suddenly darker. The high winds from the windward storm suddenly quit. Our desk lamps cast shadows out our doorways and down the linoleum-floored hallway. One by one we move to the day room at the front of the building.

Now, lonely voices of playful young men laugh, chide, and plot. We are like a pack of scraggly dogs. Men confined to intimate space revel together. We need something to do. It never takes much to divert our restless minds from study.

Someone goes out into the night and returns. "Hey, the rain's not cold," he says. Curious eyes glance at one another then to the open screen door. I jump up from the tattered lumpy couch and move outside over the wooden bridge walkway that leads to the curb. I look up into the falling waters. I open my mouth and taste it.

"Let's go see Kaimuki," I say when I return to the guys who sit in various poses upon the couches and on wooden chairs. We are dressed in shorts, jeans, and loose T shirts. Rain mutes the sound of our happy chatter. We are shoeless and quickly soaked. In loose formation we make our way down the asphalt drive to the base of the steep hill of our campus commons. A grooved concrete sidewalk feels abrasive to my softened shoeless feet. Bare feet stride through the heavy rain that falls relentlessly. Yellowed beams of headlights on passing cars illuminate the falling wet from the Pacific. Our intended destination is uphill a half mile away.

"I no like dis stuff," Ben says. He is from Maui, the son of a cattle rancher. We call him guava. He has a thick Portagee accent. "I going back."

. . . .

My Dormitory 1961

THE YEARS HAVE NOT been kind to this simply constructed wood building. It is a simple rectangle. A narrow hall runs down the center. Six rooms on one side and four the other. The building is built out over a steep cliff. From the back deck I look down onto the football field and track. The bathroom is at the back. At the front is the day room.

My room is the first one on the left. I share it with a guy from New Jersey we call Dizzy. Lloyd is cool, hip, or so he thinks. He's scatterbrained, loses his train of thought all the time and wants to be a psychologist.

I hit it off with a Hawaiian from Molokai named Larry Helm. Larry lives two doors down, can sing Hawaiian and rock and roll music, play the guitar, and party. He likes me. The feeling is mutual.

We are two of the rare non-virgins in the dorm. Most of the guys here have not only not slept with a female, but also never been drunk. Larry introduces me to the Waikiki beach boys. All are Hawaiian and love to sing, play music, and party.

. . . .

Identification 1961

ANYTHING THAT HAS YOUR name, or someone's name on it works. Pictures are for scrapbooks not driver's licenses. Somebody gives me mine. It says I was born in 1941. You only have to be 20 to legally drink in Hawai'i. If you go to some of the nastier places, you don't have to show anything but money.

Best drinking place I go to in my life is a run-down old house on the outer edge of Waikiki. It is a tiny two-bedroom old dump. How they pack over a dozen people into the living room and porch area amazes me.

Four young Hawaiian guys share the rent on this old house. Two work construction jobs to pay the bills, and two hustle tips as Beach Boys. You have to work for six weeks at a real job before you qualify for unemployment. The "unemployed two" don't get pay checks just tips. Every two months they switch roles.

They are the happiest men I ever see in my life. They hate work but gut it out so they can party all weekend. The Beach Boys get the women, and I do mean women. Plural. Some of the gals are getting a bit long in the tooth. Divorcees are easy pickings for a Saturday night party.

"Respect me," she pleads, seated on a broken sofa. Well past forty and slightly portly she is looking up at a laughing Hawaiian half her age. "You have to respect me," she slurs. She is so drunk she can't see straight.

"Eh, lady," the dark-skinned Hawaiian boy says. "I respect you, just no make me laugh, okay?" He winks, turns and begins singing while clapping his hands.

Larry picks up a guitar and gets it really going. Suddenly they're singing the Molokai theme song. This makes the women feel young again and the boys ready for sex.

· · · ·

Major and Minors 1961

I SELECT MY MAJOR BECAUSE of my freshman professor of philosophy, Howard Delaney. He comes to Chaminade from Loyola for one year. His son had died. He feels a year away from Los Angeles will be good for him and his family. Logic, Ethics, and the science of Metaphysics he presents as short, twenty-minute talks. For the remainder of the class, he speaks of his time as a lieutenant with George Patton's Third Army. The intervening fourteen years has not softened his opinion of the famous general.

Many of my freshman instructors are on sabbaticals from their schools on the mainland, or from overseas. My philosophy teacher who teaches Kant is from Germany. I do not understand her, or Emanuel Kant. I see her at Fort DeRussy beach one afternoon under a young serviceman who is a lot smaller than her. She looks like an octopus with him. This I understand.

I love the differences in my instructor's styles. It is not what they say but how they say it that most impresses or bores me. Is this a life I can aspire to? Spouting theories ungrounded in relevance for a living? Philosophy is the science of bullshit. I could do it but I would not be able to live with myself if I did it for more than a year or two.

• • • •

Dorm Games 1966

IT IS EARLY EVENING. It's been hot all day. We're playing cards in the day room. Suddenly the air feels cool. Rain runs heavily across our tar paper roof. I walk out the front door into the downpour.

"It's great outside, guys. Let's go." We decide to try skating. At the bottom of the hill next to the gym is a large concrete pad. I pour my box of laundry detergent over the pad. Barefoot we glide and slide around on the hard concrete. Laughing, falling, forgetting anything matters, we're innocent boys at play. If only life can always be so simple.

• • • •

Alea Iacta Est (The Die is Cast) 1963

I'M A MONTH SHY OF twenty when the Marines call. Two staff non-commissioned officers, local Hawai'i guys, draw my eye. They stride up the stairs to our college. Marines march when they walk together in uniform. They are given a table and two chairs in the basement of Henry Hall.

"We are looking for local boys to become Marine officers," the mix blood gunnery sergeant says to me. "President Kennedy wants the Navy and Marines more integrated."

"You got the Marine look and build," the Chinese/Hawaiian staff sergeant says with a smile.

"What do I have to do to qualify?" My question alters my life forever.

When I successfully complete two summer boot camps and graduate from college, I will be commissioned a second lieutenant in the United States Marine Corps Reserve. From there it is six months of schooling. Then, if I graduate that, I get the chance to lead Marines.

"Army Green Berets are already in Vietnam," the gunny says. "You might make it in time. We're going in for sure." (Six guys from the Hawai'i colleges join this year. Two of us are com- missioned. Jim Littler from the Mormon Church College is killed in Vietnam).

I call from the dorm. The dial phone in the day room gives no privacy. From Los Angeles Dad says: "Your mother is very upset, son." Mom might be upset but dad is not. He loves the Marines. "You'll be the first officer in the family," he says with pride.

Free will is not free. I follow my heart. My heart is not serving me. Naïve and young, I make a fateful decision that takes me on a journey I cannot control.

Once I assume the mantel of the Marine Corps, I cease being curious in school. I no longer think for myself. My future is determined. Marine is forever, they say.

I pick courses to graduate not learn. I party at every chance. I am living a life with no future other than strife in front of me.

. . . .

Quantico, Virginia Camp Upshur 1963

JULY IN VIRGINIA IS not just hot, but wet. Day and night the heat and humidity does not let up. I'm in the fourth day of boot camp. Boot camp is about chaos. Screaming, yelling, barking orders at us as we race about like panicked rats.

I'm back from the showers and trying to dress as quickly as possible. I just slip on my boxer shorts when someone yells: "Standby!" That means a drill instructor has entered our Quonset hut.

You must stop whatever you are doing and line up at attention in front of your bunk beds. You must no matter what stare straight ahead and not avert your eyes.

The drill instructor comes down the center of the squad bay that has bunk beds running down both sides of the hot metal Quonset hut. Some men are still naked. As he passes me, he pauses. Out of the corner of my eye I see him looking behind me. I feel the brim of his Smokey Bear hat touch my forehead.

"You planning on making some extra money while you're here, sweetheart?" His question startles me.

"No sir," I bark out.

"Yeah? Well, I'm gonna be keeping my eye on you," he says, then marches off.

"What the hell was that all about?" I ask in shock.

"You got your drawers on backwards," my bunkmate says.

. . . .

Together Again 1963

DAD'S INVESTMENT IN the Los Angeles liquor store pays off. They buy a new home on O'ahu with pool on the hillside above the exclusive Portlock Road.

After my sister and brother graduate from college, they too move back to O'ahu. My sister starts the Special Education program in Hawai'i. All students are bused to Waikiki and educated separately from the other students. My brother becomes a civil engineer with the City of Honolulu. Dad rejoins the company he formerly worked for called Fred L. Waldron, a food and feed distribution company.

We have four cars and four bedrooms. Everyone has a car but me. I use mom's Chevy Corvair until my brother loans me his brand-new powder blue Corvette convertible. Girls jump into that machine with power everything. I wear sunglasses when I drive it.

I don't remember having any source of income but I always have enough in my pocket to buy several $1.00 pitchers of beer and a late night $1.25 breakfast of Portuguese sausage, scrambled eggs, 2 scoops rice and white bread. I put soy sauce on the rice, catsup on the eggs, butter and guava jelly on the bread. This is Hawai'i gourmet food for a college playboy.

I feel great. Everything is wonderful. Life is beautiful. The girls, sun, surf, beach, bars, I love it all. I love it because in my heart, and certainly in my head, I know it will not last.

. . . .

Young Love 1964

IN MY SENIOR YEAR, Janell comes to Chaminade. She is from Phoenix, the daughter of an oncologist. Her parents are divorced. She's the fourth of twelve children. She is two years younger than me and innocent as a new day. I propose to her at the Pali lookout, late one night. We've known one another less than a month.

"Will you marry me?" I ask looking out into a dark, Hawai'i night.

"I guess so," she says, then begins crying. We talk the night through planning our future.

"I'm scheduled to graduate from Basic School just before Christmas, want to do it then?" My question lights her up, full bright.

• • • •

Basic School Quantico Virginia 1965

I LIVE IN THE BOQ (bachelor officer quarters). I make $300 plus a month with free room and board. I have no car and nothing to do with my money but drink after work. I am living in a section of Virginia that is semi-dry. All they can serve is 3.2% beer for a quarter a glass. The bar is conveniently just below my room on the second floor.

School is a combination of classroom and outdoor training sessions that involve "dry" and "live" firing. The best lecture I attend is on Tarawa, the WWII Marine amphibious debacle. The guest lecturer is a first sergeant who was 19 when he landed on Tarawa with the first wave of Marines.

"The Marine Corps had its head up its ass," he starts.

"You best get in quick boys, we gonna slaughter them Japs," the generals told us.

"Bullshit," he says with a sneer. "Don't trust the brass. They couldn't even get the tide right on that day." The sergeant starts pointing at us and yells: "Your job as platoon commanders is to die first, no matter who fucks up. You hear me? I love our Corps. And I mean it. You die first. That's your fucking job."

That night in the bar no one gives it notice or mention. They are all playing horse with dice, or bullshiting and laughing at scattered tables. I sit at the bar smoking a cigarette and nursing a beer. My eyes are wide open. The "first shirt's" message rings loud and clear in me.

. . . .

Infantry Commander Camp Lejeune, North Carolina 1966

I GET WHAT I WANT. I am given command of the Second Platoon of G Company, Second Battalion, Second Regiment of the Sec- ond Marine Division; I am one of 108 infantry platoon commanders in our division (10,000).

I have 44 marines who report directly to me. Our single di- vision is responsible for the Atlantic side of the Americas. At any time, we have one battalion stationed in Cuba, and one afloat in the Mediterranean. Every six months the battalion in Cuba ro- tates back to Lejeune and is replaced. When there are flare-ups in South or Central America, another battalion is sent afloat.

The battalion in the Mediterranean is gone for 18 months. We call it the Med Cruise for reason. It is considered the best tour (next to embassy duty) for an infantry marine. There are frequent port calls in Italy, Spain and the other friendly ports that rim the Mediterranean.

. . . .

Counting Men 1966

I HAVE 44 MEN I CAN actually count and over 200 that I can't. They are "part" of my platoon too. All the Marine deserters who have a home address from the eastern half of the US go onto the Second's rolls. The

Division passes names down to Regiments, then Battalions, and finally the tip of the spear, the rifle company and me.

It is just after morning formation. Our first sergeant asks to see me. He is at his desk going over a form.

"Ah, Lieutenant Spencer," he says looking up. "I've got good and bad news for you, sir."

"I'll take the bad shit first Top," I say, then light a cigarette. "You've been named defense counsel for the whole Regiment." "Ahhh, Fuck me!" I yell. "Gimme the good stuff."

"The colonel is so impressed with your qualifications he made you Regimental defense counsel," he says, and grins. I'm getting ready to throw my cigarette at him when he stops me.

"Lieutenant," he says, then waits for me to calm down, "the only good thing you can count on in this Marine Corps is when you retire with a pension." He takes a drag on his cigarette. "Otherwise, don't expect anything." I turn to leave.

"Oh, Lieutenant," he calls to me. "Don't sweat being de- fense counsel. You're expected to lose. It's all a joke."

"A joke on whom?" I say with sarcasm.

"Ooooo, look at you and the fancy language." He raises his eyebrow.

"The jokes on them dumb cowards think they can hide from us. When we find em guilty, they'll go straight to Nam. I believe they all go to infantry units."

"Makes sense to me." I say putting my cover on.

• • • •

Field Duty 1966

I SPEND THE WINTER in the North Carolina woods, chasing my fellow lieutenants around, playing war games. I feel good leading men. They follow me easily.

We are on a four-day field exercise. I have the men of second platoon, plus my share of the weapons platoon and radio operators from battalion.

At a crossroad on a dirt road, we disembark from trucks. We are in a thick forest. I am to take the right fork. The commander of first platoon takes the left fork. Third platoon will be driven to an unknown place approximately two miles away and set up defensive positions.

My order is to find and attack third platoon. First platoon must find and fight my second platoon. Our company commander rides around in his jeep with his driver and radio operator, observing only.

As soon as we disembark, I lead my platoon on a forced march moving quickly up the dirt road of the right fork. I know from my map first platoon has a longer trip to where I think third platoon will set up. All the years playing in the rain forest of Hawai'i pays off. My men are sweating and breathing hard when I stop the column short of my objective. I set up in a hidden indentation just off the dirt road. It is a perfect defensive position. I take two of my country boys and we circle in through the dense forest towards what I believe will be my prize. My lead scout crawls back to me with a big shit-eating grin on his face.

"You was right," he says softly.

Back at our second platoon I have my radio operator and my scout alone. I take the gold bars of my rank and pin them on the collars of my scout. "PFC Curtis," I say after turning him into a second lieutenant, "You and the radioman stroll up the road. When the third platoon challenges you, tell him you are from Division I.G."

"Whoopee!" Curtis goes. "I like being the inspector general."

"Okay general," I say. "Take this notebook. Make real good notes with maps. I especially want locations of the machine guns and command post."

"Lieutenant," Curtis drawls. "I'll show you where they hang their panties."

After Curtis returns with their defense positions, I brief the platoon on my plan of attack. I leave one fire team of four men to guard our packs. The rest of the squad will fake an attack at third platoon from the road. I take the rest.

We circle around third platoon through dense forest. I move them in single file using quickstep. I feel like an Indian circling his enemy. We have an hour before my decoy squad starts firing. We will attack from the opposite side of my decoy squad.

As chance would have it, our company commander is visiting third platoon when we attack.

"He cheated," the commander of third platoon says to our captain afterwards. I'm standing with Curtis who is still wearing my lieutenant's gold bars. Skipper smiles at me and shakes his head. He waves for his driver to go without saying a word.

"You're a damn cheater," the lieutenant repeats to me. "And you're a dead motherfucker," I say, blowing smoke at him with a hiss. He doesn't smoke and hates it.

• • • •

Marine Wife 1966

JANELL LOVES BEING an officer's wife. "I love it when they salute me," she says when she picks me up at our company barracks. I've spent the week in the field.

Our car has an officer's decal on the bumper. Marine guards at the main gate and enlisted men in uniform are required to salute any passing officer's car. She loves the free base activities for families. Clubs, sports and even a ceramic studio are more than she ever dreamed of having.

The only problem with this dream is with me. I know by now that I do not want this as a career. The peacetime structure is based on kissing ass. I do not do that. I am sickened by it.

We deploy to Cuba in the spring. I'll be gone for 5 months. Janell returns to her family in Phoenix.

. . . .

Safety Officer 1967

I AM PROMOTED TO FIRST lieutenant. As a second lieutenant I com- manded a rifle platoon, 81 mm mortar platoon and briefly commanded G company in Cuba.

I am now TAD (temporary duty) to the division as a range safety officer. It is a plum assignment. I work from 4 p.m. until all live firing on the base is completed. Usually, I am done by 9 p.m. If the weather is good, I play golf in the morning.

Camp Lejeune is a large base that covers miles of oceanfront and dense forested areas. Shooting and bombing is a regular, everyday thing. My job is to wait in the central command center with one radioman. If the shit hits the fan somewhere, they call me. Then, I start calling for help. I have a logbook with every number for any contingency. Marines are really good about spelling out procedures.

It is well after 9 p.m. I'm bullshitting with my radioman. We are alone in the command center. Empty desks, and their coffee cups sit idle all around us.

"When are them flyboys ever gonna finish, lieutenant?" My radioman has a Texas drawl. All the firing ranges closed hours ago. Marine A-4 Skyhawks are doing bombing runs on the outer banks. They are dropping small stuff. 250 pounders. The emergency phone rings. I grab it myself. "Hello. hello," a high panicked voice yells in my ear. "Stop the bombing. You all hear me?"

"Where are you?" I yell. "I'm working the draw bridge. A bomb almost blowed me up!" My radioman can hear the guy. He initiates a radio halt to the air officer on site. Killing Marines is one thing, but civilians? I call my commanding officer for our office at home.

He is drunk. "Ahhh sheet," he slurs. "Focking Airedales. They can't hit nothing right."

I get to see the sunrise. I wait in the office for "everyone" to show. I watch a Marine Air and Ground offensive unfurl in front of me. I love watching these career guys walking around with both hands over their ass. Nobody talks about the bridge operator. He was fine. All that sustained damaged was his underwear.

• • • •

Defense Language Institute Monterey, California 1967

I HAVE ORDERS FOR VIETNAM, but first they want me to speak Vietnamese. We rent a beautiful one bedroom furnished place, high up the hill at Pacific Grove.

I take to the language easily. I spend three months in a class of twenty. Our instructors are Vietnamese, most female. Vietnamese is a difficult language to speak. It is tonal, and one word can have as many as six different meanings depending on the pronunciation. Have you ever heard a West Virginia hillbilly speaking Vietnamese? Our teacher is a young woman who laughs like a hyena.

I get in nine holes or more, after class. Fort Ord has a beautiful golf course, one of the best I've played. I also eat a lot. My weight balloons to almost 180 lbs. I love the foghorns. I hear them at night from our place above Monterey Bay. On a still night I hear the sea lions barking too.

My wife sleeps quietly by my side as I ponder my future. Hands behind my head, I spend many sleepless nights. Am I ready?

LIFE AFTER VIETNAM - 1968 to 1986

Honolulu Airport 1968

It is just after midnight. A warm breeze and the smell of flowers envelope me as I walk down the stairs of the chartered jet. I gaze lovingly at the lights of the city off to my right. I am breathing in and out deeply, feeling slightly faint walking into the terminal.

"All Marines follow me to board buses to Pearl Harbor," a Marine at the entrance says. A U.S. Customs officer asks me,

"Anything to declare, Captain?"

"Just me," I reply.

"Welcome home," he says.

I've been traveling for three days since I left Vietnam. My wife lives twenty minutes away. Screw Pearl Harbor. I walk out of the terminal and hail a cab. I go AWOL.

"You just get back from Vietnam?" The cabby is a fat local boy.

"Yeah. Take me to Makiki," I say, then zippo a cigarette to life.

He eases the cab onto to Likelike highway and blurts out: "Eh. I just went hear, Bobby Kennedy got shot," he is looking at me in his rear-view mirror.

"What?" I ask incredulously. "What the fuck!" I yell at him. I impulsively throw my cigarette out the window.

"You okay, captain?" The cabby asks and slows down.

"Just get me home," I say, slumping back in my seat.

. . . .

Release from Active Duty

TWO DAYS AFTER I GET home, I am sitting on the balcony of our second-floor apartment, watching a palm tree wave gently in a morning breeze. I know I am not right. It is as though I am looking out at the world from inside a glass bubble. Not a month ago I was in a big-time gunfight. My gaze at the palm tree dissolves into another replay of that fight. I am home I know, but I cannot stop my mind from flashing back.

"Ernie," Janell says, standing at the sliding door. "Don't you have to check in?"

"I got less than a week left till my time's up," I say and look back at the tree.

"Come on," she says, "I don't want you getting into any trouble. Not now."

"Sure. No problem," I answer sarcastically and stand. "I'll get dressed and go down there right now."

To save four days getting home, I abandoned all my service uniforms in Okinawa. We were required to ship our service uniforms to Okinawa on our way to Vietnam.

I put on the jungle utilities that I wore home and drive to Pearl Harbor. I am directed to the S-1 administration office. It is quiet when I enter. No one seems to be working. Typewriters are still. A first sergeant sits at what appears to be the main desk.

"I'm here to get discharged," I say as I stand in front of him. He looks me over.

"You're out of uniform, captain," he responds dismissively.

"I wore this uniform all year. It's the only one I have left." I toss him my file. It is thin.

"What's this piece of shit?" He asks, staring at my file. His arrogant question sets me off. This sergeant has no Vietnam ribbons on his chest.

"It's a piece of shit cause my record book got destroyed by fire, you rear echelon motherfucker! Let's go outside. I'll whip your ass."

"Captain!" I hear a loud call from the office. I look up and it's a major.

"Let me see you in my office, now! Let me see your file," the major says as he motions me to a chair in front of his desk. His head jerks back.

"How the hell did you get three Presidential Unit Citations in one tour?"

"I was with the Twenty Sixth Marines."

"You do the siege?" He looks at me.

"Right in the bullseye," I say, nodding my head. His lips blow out in a silent whistle. He goes back to my file and flips through it.

"Why don't you go home captain and let me try to straighten this out."

"Major," I say and stand, "I got 56 days of leave pay owed me. I'm counting on that money."

"Without your record book it might take you months to resolve." I turn and as I near the door he says, "Write your congressman, captain. The Marine Corps listens to them."

God bless congresswoman Patsy Mink. I write her and receive a reply within a week. A marine general from Washington D.C. sends me a reply the following day. I get a check the next week. They are so scared shitless, two weeks later the Marine Corps sends a "final" check for 19 cents. I still have it. What an apt memento for my service.

• • • •

Starting Over 1968

TWO WEEKS AFTER I GET back from Vietnam, dad has a talk with me.

"You can't be laying around son, you have a family to take care of." I still have explosions and gunfire going off in my head. I am trying to get it together. I wish there is somewhere I could go to be alone. I am trying to come down from the insanity of Vietnam. No one else is feeling what I'm feeling. The crazy world of war has no bearing on what

I see all around me. Everyone is going about life as though there was no war. I know my guys are still getting hit. America does not give a shit about us.

"Listen to me," dad says, "The state has a program to help vets get jobs. The paper is full of want ads for people with your skills."

"Okay," I say softly in surrender, "I'll get right on it. I promise," I say respectfully.

"I'm proud of you son," dad says, looking at me with his loving eyes. "Remember. You're a Spencer. We always take care of our family."

"I will dad, best I can," I reply.

• • • •

Such A Deal - Honolulu Employment Office

THE GUY ACROSS FROM me is a middle-aged Japanese, a WWII vet- eran of the all Japanese 442nd Regiment.

"Did yooou realize, Mister Spencer," he says grinning coyly at me, "You have The three greatest job qualifications possible?" He is gay. It shows dramatically in his voice and mannerisms. Gay is accepted in Hawaii. I am not playing this guy's game, I think to myself. I just sit dead faced in front of him.

"Well...." He says, "One. You have a college degree. Two," he says raising his hand with fingers showing, "You're married." He pauses dramatically before he says, "And most important. Your service obligation is complete."

"Sounds like a hard-up economy to me," I answer.

"Yes, it is," he responds. "We're in a war time economy. That's especially good for Hawaii's economy."

"So where do I go?"

"Matson Navigation," he says immediately. "They're ex- panding beyond Hawaii.

• • • •

Modern Pirates 1968

BRED IN FETID BACKWATER ports and cities throughout the world, in crude hewn craft barely seaworthy they started. Then, trading or stealing their way upwards to ever expanding fleets of ships. They grease, steal, stall, smile, and continuously lie. Lie even when they don't have to. Streams of bullshit pour out their ears. They are the steamship owners and executives of shipping companies, today's pirates.

I go to one interview and Matson Navigation offers me a job. Right from Nam to the "world" like that. Combat to bullshit. Parading egos on review. Like some macabre collaboration between Federico Fellini and Gilbert and Sullivan, my shipping career begins.

The company has a near monopoly on shipping into the state of Hawaii. Most of the military supplies are shipped in by Matson.

"Aloooha, Matsoon," the switchboard operator purrs to incoming callers. Matson is making a ton of money. It is the height of the Vietnam War. I am what everyone wants.

Matson is a paternalistic corporation. There are no women in positions other than clerk. Women like consensus, men prefer dominance. Alpha male dogs are kinder than we humans. They let others just lick their faces.

Matson Navigation is divided into Terminal and Operations. I start in Operations, in the Traffic department. I am the Inter Island container coordinator. I run the inter-island container ship, the Matson Princess.

Matson is converting from break bulk cargo to container. When I join there are only four break bulkers left. They call at all the Island ports and at all the ports on the west coast. A break bulk ship holds the equivalent of 150 containers. It takes five days to discharge and reload a break bulker. One container crane did 30 containers per hour.

The majority of Hawaii's freight lands at Honolulu, brought in by the new container ships. The containers bound for the outside islands are transshipped on the Princess. The Princess has its own container crane on board.

I always disliked military academy types. Any man who locked himself away during his prime partying years has to be sick. Your best years get wasted marching and saluting.

All my bosses at Matson in Hawaii are academy graduates. Most are from Kings Point, the Merchant Marine Academy. But one went to Annapolis. Nosey, kiss ass, short hair, all white, first- class jerks. My immediate boss is a moron who went to The Naval Academy. Two weeks after I begin with Matson, Vietnam returns.

"I cannot find anything physiologically wrong with you, Mr. Spencer." I am sitting on the edge of his examining table, shirtless, gazing outward at him. The doctor they bring me to never asks why I might be this way. Vietnam never occurs to either of us.

An hour earlier I had collapsed with severe stomach cramps at my desk. The excruciating pain subsides there in the doctor's office.

Damn right I feel awkward taking a cab back to the office. I am too ashamed to ask anyone for a ride. Clank! The metal doors come down. Put behind. Forgotten. I am shutting my feelings off but still having trouble getting my body to go along.

"It's nothing, really, just a stomach flu," I say to Bob. Sincere is the concern in his eyes. Bob is from New England. He served in the Army just after the Korean War. Besides working for Matson, he is also a lieutenant colonel in the Hawaii Army Reserves. Hawaii is a very patriotic, flag waving state.

"Sheat Ernie, the closest I ever came to combat was those bath and massage houses over on Okinawa - hee hee." A wheezing hiss marks his self-generated laugh, obviously his attempt to draw me out.

I ain't war rapping with a chain smoking, never saw shit doggie, I say to myself.

"I'm fine Bob, you're the one who needs help." We both laugh. He is one of the few management people at Matson who is compassionate. I like Bob.

Within the month Bob and I are sitting alone in his cubicle, chairs near each other. He sighs openly then slowly almost inaudibly speaks.

"My daughter and I went to identify him today. They were married less than a year. My granddaughter is only two months old. She'll never know her father. He was a Navy corpsman who volunteered. He was a local boy. He hit a booby-trapped artillery round while on patrol with the marines. I hope my daughter gets on with her life." He sighs heavily. I say nothing.

Passively we gaze to and away from one another. Traffic flows by on the busy boulevard. Through thin curtained large glass walls, we see the traffic outside our ground floor office. For countless minutes we sit watching. Silence fills the air. Bob needs to tell the story of the dead. I do have a lot of recent experience with that. Why do they always think that I need, or want to know? Maybe they know I will understand.

Two Marines I know are buried at Punchbowl National Cemetery. I cannot bring myself to attend their burials. I read their obituaries in the evening paper and say nothing to my wife. I do not cry. I do not scream. I do not talk about the anger and confusion I am feeling. I shut myself down. Deliberately. I am ashamed of myself, for surviving.

I am trying as hard as I can to forget. It is late night. I am in bed, soaked in sweat. I grind my teeth. I look over at my wife asleep. I get up. Walk to the living room, then out onto the balcony. I feel the warm tropical breeze. I smell the night air. I remember something my best buddy Ken said. We were having a cigarette after a gunfight in Leatherneck Square.

"Spence," he started, "It's either gonna be okay, or it's not. We're just here for the ride." Then, I gaze up at the dark shadow of the mountain. I take several deep breaths, walk back in and get back in bed. I am only twenty-five. I have a long road ahead. I know that I alone must fix whatever it is that is ailing me.

• • • •

New Life 1969

I HAVE A SENSE OF PURPOSE. I not only have a wife, but a daughter. I endure the corporate world for my family's sake. I suck it up and go to work every day, rain, or shine. I am promoted to Fleet Superintendent, charged with scheduling all ships coming and going to Hawaii. One ship backed up anywhere impacts all the ship's schedules moving forward. Berths have to be scheduled precisely. Amounts of cargo, available labor, space limitations on shore, all impede the schedule.

I am already being "looked at," by the big bosses in San Francisco. My fast, accurate assessments are accepted without question. Only my moron boss, the Annapolis graduate, questions me.

"Tell me what is wrong with your plan," he always starts.

"I don't know the weather." That response works.

• • • •

Family Dreams 1970

MY SISTER IS MARRIED, my brother and I have children. We gather most weekends at mom and dad's house. Once again mom leads the family. I see it on her. She and dad love being with their children and grandchildren. Mom is obsessively in love with my daughter. Men sit out back and talk hunting and fishing. Women chat inside while tending the children.

Who exactly comes up with the hair-brained idea, I do not recall. The greatest enthusiasts though are my brother and brother-in-law.

Both are engineers and hate their jobs. Dad is the traffic manager at Fred L. Waldron; Dad and the new president of his company do not get along. The Hawaii general manager says I can expect a transfer to Matson's headquarters within a year. I would rather stay in Hawaii than play the corporate game. Dad makes it easy for me.

I have no money to invest. I came home from Vietnam with nothing saved. My wife had spent everything.

. . . .

Canada Venture

MY BROTHER IS THE FIRST, a choice that is expected. That is the Spencer way. I honor and do what daddy and mom want. I would not do that today.

Daddy got "down-sized." He is at that age and time, middle age, when such an event is devastating to a man's ego. Bless daddy though, he ends up forgiving the man who does him and lasts (perhaps by chance) until the man dies before daddy.

This Canada adventure starts sometime in late 69 or early 70. Daddy has no problem convincing Bill. Ray and Betty heartily agree. Bill and Ray base their decision on the location and what it has to offer. Wonderful fishing, hunting... up to moose. Deer are everywhere. Same with the migrating ducks, geese. Pheasant year round. Grouse and on and on. That is what attracts those two dreamers, Bill, and Ray. Me? Daddy does not ask. He tells me that he and "your mother," how he refers to her when talking directly to me, a Spencer thing, want me to help start it. Tooty and young Evie go too. It is my mom's dream for her children to come together and live on for the rest of her life in peace and harmony.

. . . .

Canada 1970

I STAY OUT OF THE SEARCH for "the promised land." The other three males do the recon. First, they tried northern California. Dad loves fishing and wants to go to McCloud, near Mount Shasta. It is not financially viable. It is my brother-in-law from British Columbia who leads us to Woods Lake. "We not only fish, but hunt too," Ray says.

"Ern, I need you and your family to help start the business in Canada." dad says to me on the phone. That's his pitch. The Marine son leads the way.

I am not happy with the corporate environment. What the hell do I have to lose? I give Matson two weeks' notice in writing. They let me go that same day. San Francisco does not tolerate disloyalty.

My parents buy a little summer resort on a small lake in the Okanagan Valley, British Columbia, Canada. We do it legally. We sell almost everything we have, the car, furniture, clothing, and toys. Four adults and one toddler cross the border at Osoyoos, B.C. in 1970. We are all in one car.

"Even if you move back to the states, you're Canadians for the rest of your life," the customs officer says in a practiced way. Wow. All it takes is proof we have a real gig waiting for us in Canada. We have bought a summer resort on a lake with our American dollars. Dad shows them the papers. We are allowed in and receive Canadian legal immigrant status.

Sam's Resort becomes my home for the two summers and one winter that I live in Canada. The tourist season is short in Canada. You only have a couple of months of hard work before the leaves change color and the birds start migrating south. I hate the cold but love the winter there on Woods Lake.

The resort is on a lakefront. The back is a camp spot shaded by kind, gentle willow branches. Ample shade they make for the small trailers, or tent cabins. No sewage hook-ups, but water and electricity.

It is the height of the tourist season. My brother Bill freaks out just trying to be the fry cook behind our breakfast and lunch counter. Lucky for us Ray and Betty never come.

Bill and Carol last less than a month before they take their two young sons and fly home to Hawaii. Some fight between Tooty and Carol sparks it all. Carol has the good financial sense to see that it isn't going to work. I don't even remember what it is about, but I am personally glad to see them leave.

By now dad is savvy enough to realize the resort cannot support the whole family. I see that based on the gross income after that first short (hard) tourist season.

· · · ·

Echo Lake 1970

MY FAVORITE PRIVATE pastime is fishing. During the summer I fish tiny reservoirs nearby. It is the busy time in our resort business. Good trout fishing lakes the locals say are up in the mountains, rising boldly from the Eastern side of the Okanagan Valley in which we live. The start of the Canadian Rockies. On the ridges and mountains beyond, thousands of pristine, isolated lakes.

Fly on a float plane is the only practical way in for most. With four-wheel high-powered trucks some challenge the mountain range to lakes allowing six-pound Kokanee trout to be taken on flies, hand tied. Kokanee, a rainbow trout of lustrous sheen, sparkling tiny scales spraying outward, yellows, blacks, reds dotting its flashing sides. With passion rarely seen in men's eyes in these parts, old man Willet relives the drama of the mammoth trout he hands me as a present from his fishing trip. As though passing the tradition of that noble being, he passes that fish's legacy on to me. A memory.

When time allows that fall, I drive up to Echo Lake. Up the highway north an hour to the town of Lumby. An old-time logging town. Just past town I hang a right onto a fourteen-mile winding slowly rising mountain range dirt road. Suddenly I drop into a narrow cut, a valley. Trees angle in plumb to the sharp climbing hillside bank. Flashes I see. Water blinking, winking at me, blown by the gusts rolling over the clear, flat surface, leaving a trail of rippling waves.

As in the shell of the conch, when at lake level I hear the sounds ricochet. That haunting almost plaintive howl of the loon. At dusk it sings to its mate. The loon crying out its place in this idyllic setting. Its voice fills the valley. Echoes resound or whispers play.

Boy, can I hear the echoes. Impulsively I yell "hello!" Sec- onds later I hear a recording of myself the way I really sound. If the wind is still, I hear the quiet conversations of other fishermen across the five hundred yards to the other side.

Over clear visions on bottoms of sand or green weeds rising straight up, on a canoe we glide. Fifty feet or better straight down I can see. Breathtaking clarity. No color to such water when viewed this way. Perfect.

Too far for tourists and too small for the locals. Trout don't grow big here. Locals say it is because the water is too clear, not enough food.

Echo Lake freezes hard every winter. Silvery thin and soft are those trout in the spring. Voracious but gaunt from the black freeze.

Ah, but in October just before it starts to freeze, those that were so thin three months earlier are robust, stout, and strong from long days of bright sunlight. Close to the shore the old timers lay.

Fly casters cannot always get in close to the shore where the big trout lay. Trees and brush line the shore where we cast. I am a spin caster. Flicking lures to within inches of the shore is my specialty. With a reed thin rod and mini reel, I nail them. A lure of silver shining metal on one side and convex on the other a burnt orange iridescent. A treble hooked lure, tiny, deadly.

"Hey, that's not fishing, eh." The 'eh' sounds like a long a. Ray pouts at me from the back of the canoe as we sit facing one another. He has yet to have a strike on any of his hand tied flies.

"You get yours your way, I get mine, mine." I slowly pace out the words for him. Just the wrist. Like a short forehand in ping pong. A slight chop. Arching, the lure shoots from the end of the pole, right for the shoreline. Trailing line following. Under the low hanging branches near water's edge trout lay under the branches waiting for things to drop. Bugs, seeds, anything. Last chance to feed while food is falling. Too soon the clang of cold sealing, pushing all below down, encased. The lure just hit when a flash, splash, zing, he hits it. Straight at me some fifty feet off- shore he comes. Deep water he seeks. My hands jerk before my face as I try to bring him up. If he gets to the weeds, he will be lost. Pump, reel and pull back. Slack a moment, then flash again. He breaks water. Turn him one last time and he comes in easily. In clear view forty feet away, he wavers in. The lure rudely leads him toward me. Green threaded net dips to meet him. Up quickly I flop him on the floor before me. His speckled spots are brightened by the overhead sun. A few last smacks of his tail and body twists and it is over.

"Like I said Ray, you get yours your way, I'll get mine, mine. Well, if you don't mind, why don't you drop me back off at the camp. I've got my limit."

• • • •

CANADA WINTER SCENE 1970

IT FEELS HEAVIER TODAY, absent the light, crisp cold, usually felt here in the interior. A low-pressure system prevails. Soon black, laden clouds move in. It snows by nightfall. It's what the weatherman predicted that morning. Steam streams out my nostrils. Wide open spaces everywhere. Sunlight hits everything just right. Whiteness of winter engulfs me. Soft, pillowy snow all over the place. Piled randomly. Careful dollops smoothed exactly right against the outcroppings of rock, or up against that small stand of thin, bare trees. Unimposing birch, naked without its summer sheen of flashing, waving greens. Winter limbs. Skinny arms so withered, press skyward in surrender.

My vision drifts over the natural lift of the ridge on which I stand. On a snowmobile up an old logging trail, I have come. Bounding snow drifts, miles up into nowhere. Before me, snow blends into a light blue sky. I look down into the valleys on either side. Blues to grays to sharp white, stroke outward. Painted onto and over the land. Exposed and in shadow. It has hushed the earth.

Snow. Tender silence. Lightly flailing birch branches in the distant tree line. A sudden cooling kisses the right side of my face. Smoothly and cooler the wind swirls by, touching my bare hand, across my face, and into my ear. The static of wind in my ear. Whispering winds. Silently I stand gazing outward. Cold air passes inward with each breath. Small clouds end each cycle of breath from my life. Beauty draws me inward into myself.

I have endless time to myself, alone. There is great stillness and quiet. I use rubber overshoes and thick wool socks. This gives my Hawaii feet the insulation they need. I walk for hours on the frozen lake, or over snowdrifts. I relax here. There is no war. I realize my problem is being with other people. I do not respect most people. I only know their shallow sides. I do not know them intimately. I do not trust. I do not care.

I know after that first summer the resort cannot support two families. Dad compounds the problem by building cabinettes, his term, on the prime camping spots down near the lake. He reasons that the space will generate more income that way than with a tent camper. He is wrong. No one wants to use his hot cabins in the summer and pay for them.

My mother is the happiest I have ever known her, so is dad. Mom spends endless hours with my young daughter. Dad loves being with me, working on things together. I learn carpentry, plumbing and electrical. It is what he had done with his father. I love my father. I never hear him express love for anyone, but he does for certain music, and food.

• • • •

Johnny Jack 1970 Canada

"JOHNNY JACK HERE." The Indian talks into our phone. He's swaying, rocking back and forth. His wild, drunk eyes fixed into nowhere staring straight ahead. He jerks himself upward trying to keep himself from falling over. The phone at his ear keeps dropping down. He steps forward and back, rocking. Booze hits me with gusts as he breathes outward.

It is after one in the morning when his wife comes to our door with the baby. She has to bang really hard since it is blowing cold snowy wind. The door is below our upstairs bedrooms. The six-month-old baby looks deathly. I call the hospital. I tell the nurse that I am seeing a real sick little baby. She wants to talk to the father since the mother is too drunk to be lucid. I trek out to the cabin to get Johnny. I drag his drunken ass out of bed. He is in his long johns. I half carry him as he staggers in his unlaced boots to our place and the phone.

"Johnny Jack here," he repeats. He listens with deadened eyes a few moments then blurts out, "I don't really know, my baby's just very sick. The baby's been sick for about a week." Swaying, he stands gazing into oblivion. After several moments he hands the phone to me.

It is the hospital nurse, "Can you bring the baby in?" She is curt and pissed.

Great I think to myself, I'll get taken for an Indian again. I've grown my hair down over my shoulders. Many people think I am an

Indian. I drive the 14 miles into Kelowna to the hospital. I am dressed in a checkered wool shirt, long hair down to my shoulders. I feel like an Indian. It is my hippie period.

During the summer I see the Indians out in the fruit orchids picking apples, pears, and cherries. They live in flimsy shacks adjacent to the orchards. There is an Indian reservation nearby. They are the most poorly constructed buildings in the entire area. The locals do not think much of the Indians. Canadians seem very open minded on racial issues with the exception of their own native inhabitants. Indians weren't allowed to purchase liquor in British Columbia until recently.

A friend whose folks own the town grocery tells me of a drunk Indian reeking of vanilla who plops a gallon jug of clear white liquid vanilla down on the counter next to the register.

"Going to make a big cake," he smiles through a face of missing teeth. Vanilla. Vanilla is what they use as a substitute for booze. They sell the Indians vanilla instead of booze.

On payday, I see Indians in white man's bars in town drinking their liquor. I want to put alcohol in the Canadian's cake mix and blow up their racist asses.

Johnny and his buddies are just like old line Marines. Both could blow an entire paycheck in one night of drinking. Fall ass down, drunk. Johnny Jack comes riding home some paydays in a taxi, all the way from town where he works at the lumber mill. He staggers out, a case of Canadian logger under an arm. Next to his chest he clutches a solitary sack of groceries, obvious the packet of hot dog buns. They feast that night. He's had at least a couple of hours at the tavern. His frame is squat and husky. His ever-present green and black wool shirt guards him against the frozen wind.

He pushes outward towards his cabin. Freezing Arctic winds whip a lock of hair over his flushed oval face, with wide, black eyes and mouth dotted black with teeth missing. Slivers of ice hang on his eyebrows.

For but a moment his face clears and becomes dignified. Then swaying and staggering, he hoots and howls a high war cry, announcing his arrival. The lord and master is home.

"Are you related to these people?" the nurse coolly asks, ever so slight her condescending tone and look. We are at the hospi- tal, the three Jacks and me.

"No. I am not!" I inflect in a harsh, rude manner.

The nurse who examines the baby is tender to the child, but not the parents. She calmly explains the nature and treatment for the child's pneumonia. They will keep the baby for several weeks.

"Too bad the baby couldn't be hospitalized longer," she says to me. "They cannot adapt. That's their problem. It is not just the liquor." Her eyes avert mine. Canada has socialized

medicine. No medical insurance worries. Johnny has free health care.

We let the Jacks rent one of our small cabins near the lake. It is a summer cabin and unheated except for a small propane stove. The cabin offers scant protection from the blasts of cold off the frozen lake. Awful, frozen weather comes when the Jack's baby gets sick. My god they are filthy. Their cabin is two small rooms and a tiny bathroom, hooked to a small septic tank. The toilet backs up constantly. It costs us twenty bucks a pop to have it pumped. The propane costs us more than the rent. The rent is always late.

"I spend a lot of money on booze," a sober Johnny confesses during a lighter moment. He sounds like a man talking about medals earned in battle, or tough jobs done. Johnny Jack is doing his time. Indian way. He is a year or two older than me. I am 26. Johnny is the head of his clan. He often has cousins or aunts living with his family. All in that little two room cabin. It is the best housing they can get. We feel sorry for them.

They butcher deer right outside the cabin. That is what they eat most of the winter. Indians can hunt or fish any time of year. No license. No limit. The local white Canadians resent that.

Johnny and his family get to be too much. He and his family are told to leave. Sad.

It is early springtime. The Jacks are long gone. Splashing in the lake to the side of our beach I see Johnny's son, and older sister. The boy is eight or nine, the girl eleven or twelve. A pale blue sky paints the day clear and sunny. Two months have passed since they moved. Wherever it was, they survived. The kids are giddy and laughing as they splash about in the cold water of our lake. Laughing. Splashing. Winter long forgotten.

I think the baby girl lived, that year anyway.

• • • •

Checking Out 1972

THE SECOND SEASON IS a financial disaster. Canada is in a recession. Dad's cottages do not rent. All our spare capital is lost. I can count. I know that this "family business" is a bust.

When daddy's 'cabinettes' building venture proves a business bust the next season I know it's over. He knows it is over. He tells me "we" can't afford for Tooty and Evie and me to live there.

"I'm sorry son," he sadly says when he tells me. He cannot look me in the eye when he says that. Shame, sadness, pain he feels.

"What will you Tooty and Evie do? Your mother and I hope you can somehow stay."

"You fucking kidding me daddy? Me? I'm a survivor, re- member?" A vicious sneer becomes my face.

Dad kept up on the news from Hawaii. Seatrain Lines, an east coast outfit, has started container service to Hawaii from the west coast. The president, Frank T. had been Matson's sales manager when dad was the traffic manager for Fred L. Waldron in Hawaii. Dad calls Frank. I am offered a job without an interview.

"Take the car, son," dad says. "When you get there, you'll work in sales. I know the sales V.P. at Seatrain from his days with Matson in Hawaii." Dad is so matter of fact. He doesn't ask me what I want.

I love the solitude in Canada. I can relax here when I am alone. All I want now is to be alone. I know something is terribly wrong with me. Vietnam is always with me. Nightmares are a regular part of my life. But here, I can shake them off. Whether walking, or fishing, when alone I feel safe.

I get a gig with one letter to a guy I used to work with at Matson. So low and behold, I begin the worst time of my life. I get a job back in shipping and off we go to Oakland and shipping for sixteen hard years. Working that gig makes me flat ass nuts. Running. Fucking. Eating. Running up to eighty miles a week. Bedding five or more women at a time. I have no idea how the fuck I did that gig. 1972 to 1985 was crazy. Everybody was fucking crazy. At least the ones I knew.

• • • •

September 1972

IT IS EARLY AFTERNOON when I reach the San Francisco Bay on its eastern side. I stop at a motel in Albany and rent the place for a week. I have been driving for almost a day without sleep. I am buzzed with energy. I start smoking again on the drive down.

The hardest part about starting is the disgusting taste it leaves in my mouth. I need to walk before I find a place to eat.

The sun starts to set as I walk out onto the Berkeley pier. The water is calm, windless. Gulls circle searching for one more score. The Golden Gate bridge looks black with the sun behind it.

What is happening to me? I feel used. I would rather be a whore than do what I am about to do: be a salesman. I will not be selling a product, something tangible. I'll be selling bullshit. My life is not mine. It never has been. When will I ever be free to be me? I am just the family clown who makes everyone else laugh. My life is a cruel joke. It's dark when I get back to my car.

I find a burger place. Three days later my wife and daughter arrive on a bus. We start our lives over again from scratch.

• • • •

Busy Body Oakland 1972

"HEY, YOU'RE ERNIE SPENCER, right? Don Brazil. I'm Don Brazil." His suited arm swings at me like a log. Slow, palm open, hand extended to shake mine. His head tilts: he has a phony ass grin on his face.

Come on, Jesus Christ, why me? I get that premonition my first minute on the job. The secretary has just shown me to my desk in the salesmen's corner. Bullshit city. First clown to hit me up is a puke. I smell him right off. Nam gave me that nose.

"Understand you used to work at Matson?" His eyes wide, he searches me. "What have you been up to the past year or two?"

"Yeah, Don, is it? I've been fishing up in Canada and mostly minding my own business. How about you?"

"Don't be so touchy, guy," he taunts me, "in case you don't know it, I'm probably going to be your boss."

I take a step backward expecting trumpets to blare and a drum roll. This has to be a candid camera show. This guy has to be a joke they are playing on me. In Nam he would not have lasted one night. Frag bait.

Dandy Don is real as hell. Fortunately, he never does become my boss. He worms, sniffs, and barges his way in on everything. What is it that possesses someone to ever want to know that much trivial junk about others? Well, what the hell, some people collect stamps.

• • • •

The Wild West

I'M GIVEN A $2,500 cash advance, a company car, and an unlimited expense account. My accounts vary from liquor to car tires, jams, candies, and coffee. My territory stretches from Salinas to San Francisco.

I start drinking scotch in San Francisco with a woman who imports and distributes it. The first time we have lunch I get so loaded I have to sleep in my car for several hours.

At the office I sit at my desk getting my expense account ready. I am told to spend as much as possible. Seatrain Lines has a cost-plus contract with the US government. We make twenty percent on top of all expenses. The war in Vietnam is paying for everything. We are expanding into Europe even though Europe has nothing to do with our war. The war is winding down, men are coming home. We are entering a recession.

Like the young nymphet being broken in by her pimp, Don counsels me one day.

"Hey Spence, my man, you're making us all look bad, ole buddy?" Silently my gaze meets his darting snake-like eyes. Seeing no response on my part, he continues. "Your expense account is too low man."

"What's too low Don?" my challenge fires back.

"Mine is more than three times yours."

"So maybe you and your produce shippers eat more than my accounts. Maybe you like padding, I don't."

"You'll never make it in sales Spence, mark my word." Razor sharp is his look, smiling.

Sandy is our secretary. She's perky cute, in her early twenties, from Iowa and goes with a guy in the Coast Guard. As I drop my expense account into her in-box she says,

"My boyfriend just went on a two-month deployment. Wanna have a drink tonight?" She blinks big eyes and flashes a full smile. When a woman looks at me that way, I know she has more than a drink in mind.

"Maybe some other time," I say politely.

"Well, okay, but don't make me wait too long." Within the month I take her up on her offer.

Our company has a reputation in Oakland. Parties are held almost every week in our large spacious atrium with a glass ceiling. Members of the Oakland Raiders football team are frequent guests. Seatrain is known for having good looking young available women employees. The men are your run of the mill collection of jerks and ambitious kiss asses. Casual affairs are a way of life.

The last time I lived in California the girls would not dance with me because of my looks. Now they want to sleep with me just so they can say they've had Asian.

I know I am doing wrong. My wife and daughter are innocent. I am lost in this way of life. I'm surviving the best I can. This is not enjoyable at all. It's horrible. I drink and screw around to forget it. But I cannot hide from my nightmares. The night sweats haunt me. I have Post Traumatic Stress Disorder and don't even know it.

• • • •

Coffee

I DEVELOPED THE HABIT in Vietnam. Coffee cut the taste of the bad water. I am driving into Salinas. It's nine in the morning. I notice an open bar and pull into the parking lot. Inside it is musty bar stink. The bartender greets me with a nod. At the end of the bar sits a grungy, longhaired guy who stares at his beer. Bars open at six, so he is probably into his second or forth.

I left my coat in the car, but I am still too overdressed for the place.

"Can I have a coffee if you have it?"

"Just made some," the bartender replies. "Black?"

"Yes, thank you." I nod. My tie hits the bar as I take a stool.

"I know you from somewhere," I hear him. I turn on my barstool to face him. His face is worn and deeply creased. His hair unwashed and scraggly. His eyes are lifeless. This is what one looks like when perpetually drunk.

"The man's just here for some coffee," the bartender interjects, cutting him off. "He's not here to talk about the war, Curtis. Pay him no mind," the bartender says as he places the white cup filled with black before me. "He's a sick Vietnam vet," he whispers into my face.

I say nothing; just sit quietly, taking slow sips. I stay fifteen minutes, then lay a ten-dollar bill on the bar.

"Buy him a drink or two," I say, stand and leave without looking back.

Outside the bright morning sun and fresh clean air wash over me. As I drive down to my meeting at Firestone Tire, I feel the Voice from Vietnam say without words: "He is my son."

After Firestone I call on Smucker's Jams, then have lunch with the traffic manager of Peter Paul Almond Joy candy.

All day I cannot shake the image of the drunk. "I know you from somewhere," was not a question. That drunk recognized me. I feel the hair on the back of my neck go up as I approach the bar on the way out of Salinas. I am breathing deeply and clammy as I drive by it. I fear if I stop, I might change. I fear change more than where I am. How stupid is that?

I am depressed and do not realize it. Many a night I lie awake smoking in bed. I am filled with a tense energy that does not abate.

I do not drink at home but do everywhere else. I often drive through the Caldecott tunnel bombed out of my mind. The white dashes mark the lanes that guide me on a flight path home. If I didn't have a wife and baby, I would drive far into America and lose myself. I resent my family. I hate being me and the position I'm in. I am fucked.

Promises aren't working for me. Marriage, family, work obligations are a trap. I accept these social rules as a vital part of life itself. I do not see the possibility of any other way. On many a night I lie awake smoking in bed while my wife sleeps. The despair I feel claws at me. I stare at the ceiling wide awake and dread the coming day.

I hate everything I'm doing. I wish I did not feel, but I do. Waves of dread wash over me as I drive into work. I walk into a surreal world of jabbering fools laughing at their own stupidity.

• • • •

Directing People

MY TIME IN SALES ENDS when they realize I am better at directing people than selling dreams to gullible customers.

Documentation connects everything. Ships, trucks, trains all wait until they have the forms they need to proceed. Original bills of lading are legal tender. Goods move from origin to destination governed by their bills of lading. A piece of paper stamped and signed "original", or its certified copy moves everything in international trade. A given shipment can be scattered in numerous individual ocean containers. That shipment does not move unless all parts are accounted for. We begin to use trains to move containers coming from the Far East to their destinations on the East Coast of the United States. Bypassing the Panama Canal our ships cycle on one coast instead of two. If those containers have not cleared U.S. customs, In Transit custom documents need to be prepared and checked by U.S. customs officers.

• • • •

Little Johnnie and His Wonder Boys - Oakland 1975 to 1981

"HI, I'M JOHN GRAVES." Puffed out chest. Outstretched hand waiting to shake anything that moves in front of him. Plastic grin. He is short. Like a lot of other short guys with money he draws more attention to himself by dressing too in, too sharp. Jolting handshakes, back slaps, loudness, the obnoxious "Ha, Ha" punctuates most of his statements. Johnnie is hot property in the shipping business.

After the last management group, it isn't hard for anyone to look good. Raped and pillaged by the East Coast truckers who ruin Seatrain, we are ready for a change.

"I. I. I." You hear that a lot from Johnnie. "Want" usually follows. Shipping is always affected by market forces well beyond the sphere of influence of something as insignificant as a shipping company. Pirates are a dime a dozen. Johnnie sells dreams, bullshit.

He loves traveling throughout the Orient, his domain, now as President of Seatrain Pacific, our latest name. Morals Johnnie lacks completely. Get him drunk and laid, that's what little Johnnie wants. Male or female they say about Johnnie. Orient can get you laid and little Johnnie loves Asian women. One of his many Asian secretaries tells me that. Johnnie is always trying to get her to go to bed with him. She isn't that kind of woman.

I am her lover. I laugh my ass off when Johnnie calls her at night, and I am there. Men make such asses of themselves begging and pleading. I do get a different perspective on him that way.

A slight rasp to his voice from smoking constantly, Johnnie is only forty-five. If he isn't alcoholic, he sure fakes it well. At every chance it is booze. A wet bar is always well stocked next to his office. Liquor is served with the slightest provocation. A new moon.

"Ha, Ha," he grins like a surprised jackass. Little Johnnie roams the room, glass in hand, scotch, ice. Don't worry about penetrating questions or stimulating conversation with little Johnnie. During one of our parties, I hear him ask a guy who works for me, "Well, how's the wife and kid?"

Straight faced as hell Alloy responds, "Oh my daughter's fine, but my wife died a month ago. Remember?"

Oh! Well good job. Ha, Ha." Exit idiot, stage left. A moment later he is off into another round of spreading his magic, laughing. "Aren't we having fun?"

Tacky. That is the essence of Johnnie. Presents. He loves presents more than a kid at Christmas. Every year Johnnie's boys take up a collection for Johnnie's very own Christmas present. While everyone else gets a little box of jam, Johnnie gets something worth a couple thousand dollars. The jam is mailed to your home. "From Johnnie," it says. Cheap Johnnie charges it to the company.

"I don't imagine you'd care to pitch in on John's present?" I never help pay for his present.

My boss is a repatriated, sloven, Englishman. His accent adds a certain Continental charm, Johnnie feels. Too bad I never have the chance to work with an intelligent one.

"My, your wisdom does amaze me, Robin," calm, I retort to his request for a donation for Johnnie.

"Piss off, you miserable bastard," he snaps. Best chain to jerk is British. So reserved, dignified. To get them snarling, vile. Marvelous. Sweet smile, right edge of my mouth slowly rises.

Johnnie and I always get along just fine.

"Hold on for Mr. Graves," a secretary says. Another sign of domination. Guys in shipping love to play power games. To have to hold while someone else has their secretary call you is a sign of lower status, for you.

"Ernie, my man, can you get my car cleared down to the ship? I want to park next to the what do you call stairs?"

"Gangway, John. It's called a gangway. I'll see that they let you drive through the terminal."

Another drunken feast and party given onboard a cargo vessel. Parties onboard cargo vessels are tacky. No room. Out of the small dining room guests spill. Down narrow corridors. Foul odors vent from crewmen's rooms.

"Ha, Ha, this is great!" Johnnie beams, flushed with exuberance, the look of one who has just scaled a peak. We stand next to the ships rail, looking out across the channel, the sun dying behind the distant San Francisco skyline.

"Well, I'll see you later John." I turn to leave. I had stopped by the party moments earlier for appearances sake.

"Wait, wait, wait. Show me back to the main dining room first. I need another drink."

Gulls delicately swing into their landings. Others perch on the low rails at piers edge. The vessel rests. It is between work shifts. The large container gantry cranes lay silent.

Laughter drifts down from above. As I walk slowly on the dock away from the party I wonder if that clown even ties his own shoes.

• • • •

Janet, 1972

JANET WAS A HIPPIE when I was in Vietnam. She is a Dutch farm girl from Washington who ran away to the free lifestyle of S.F in 1967. We meet in 1972 when she transfers from Seattle to the Oakland office that I work in. She knows I am married.

The first time I make love to her, I want to leave. She is eight years younger than me and into free love. Not that she is promiscuous, sport fucking is prevalent in the early seventies. By the time I meet Janet I have pretty much slept with all the available women in our office.

My relationship with Janet is kept secret. Though we work together, we hide our living arrangement. My company even pays to move her and my wife and daughter at the same time.

Addictions are all about secrets. In 1973, I move in with Janet. I also go full blown PTSD. The intensity of that illicit, secret relationship with Janet fuels the fires of my lost emotions. I begin painting to vent my powerful feelings. I still do not relate it to Vietnam. I am fine, I think. I have a good job.

Janet leaves in 1977. I have worn her out. She wants a committed relationship. "Either or," she confronts me. "Or" I choose.

We remain close friends. Janet tries marriage and fails. She has a son. I have only fond memories of Janet. We watch ourselves age by seeing one another throughout the ensuing years.

• • • •

Wonder

WONDER IS NOT ONE OF those things that is easily comparable. You can't go around measuring your degree of wondering with that of others. We seem to like to be able to measure. Starts real young, too.

"My dad can beat up your dad." We're so stacked up against everything. Scored.

"Mrs. Spencer, Ernest is not doing that well in math." Yes, but he can play and fool around to beat the band. I was one of those kids who liked to wonder about things. In our time no one admits to things like that. John Wayne didn't think. People did things they didn't think about.

Wonder is my world. Wondering about the world. Why, why, why? Why this, why that. No one gives me that. That is all mine. Society gives me standards. Measurement.

The problem with wondering is that it makes you question things. That's the most dangerous thing you can do. You suffer when you do that. Oh, when you're young it's fun and all. Inno- cent bewilderment. Everything is so fresh through eyes so young.

When you get older wondering lets you see the possibilities, but old reality has been with you awhile by then. Sitting so close to you that you start getting calloused from it.

Who are the slaves and who are the free? Driving those twenty miles every morning to that job I absolutely detest, I wonder. I mentally step out and sit up on the hillside beside the freeway. Watching myself inside this metal shell I drive. Jockeying constantly for position with others in their metal shells. Measured even there. Smug looks, like my Mercedes beats your Chevy.

Don't you see what a danger you are to yourself and society when you act in such a way? My god, what happens if everyone does that? People might change. They might not buy the Madison Avenue spiel anymore. We've got to work. We've got to be measured, quantified, and graded. There must be differences or society won't work.

You know I've been thinking about this since I've been back from Nam anyway, probably even before. What fries my ass is that they're right. Society won't work without our standards. We've got to be moral as they say. We've got to constantly judge, agree, or whatever.

That's the heartache of the wonderer, there's nowhere else to go. I mean how many worlds are there? Some days I sit out on the hillside all day while the rest of me goes to work. That's lone- some man. Sitting out there and knowing that this society, the way it is, can't handle me. I have nowhere else to go.

• • • •

Anger - 1978

"BE COOOOL. BE WISE. Be beautiful." The voice of the black DJ is deep and throaty as I listen to the radio on the way to a job I hate. Black men are beautiful. The world can be absolutely shitting on them, and they still make it on what they got. Soul brother. No white man is going to take away the brothers' dignity.

I am deeply in the corporate white man's world. More and more my feelings move towards the outsiders. They have my body, but not my soul. I want my dignity. I have lost my dignity. It is my dignity, damn it. I have lost my dignity. I am torn between my sense of duty to my family and my inner desire. My anger owns me. I am barely hanging on, just surviving. Making the best of it. Tell me a better way? I would ask myself, but never listen. My anger is not about listening, or reasoning. My anger is about reality. I am not bullshitting when I am angry. Long gone are the whys. No need to question any longer.

This is the world I came home to. This is the world that let me tell myself day after day for over a year, in Nam "It don't mean nothin." I fought a war denying myself the true reality in order to come back to this. I blame myself and that is why I am so pissed off.

What would it be like if I had married Janet, and not listened to dad? I know better, I really don't need this. I just don't want to fight anymore.

Man, oh man where in the hell can I Chu Hoi? (surrender)

· · · ·

Terri, 1979 – 1983

TERRI COMES ON STRONG to me. We are meant to be adversaries. We work for the same company, but for different departments. Office intrigue I find boring. She's been sent to work at the terminal to keep an eye on me. I guess she likes what she sees. She appeals to my senses. She feeds me and loves me like no one else. She's neurotically possessed by me. Her father is also a womanizer.

I am ashamed of what I do with Terri. Not about my promiscuity and screwing around on her, but about education. I help pay her way through law school. The deal is that no matter what our future relationship, she will always be my attorney. She does not honor that contract. After she flunks the bar the second time, she stops seeing me.

She might not be licensed by the bar to practice, but she sure seems like a lawyer when she dumps me. I am at the height of my legal problems when she kisses me off. For Christmas in 1983 she gives me a cold goodbye. I am amazed watching that same face that screamed in ecstasy so many times before now turn to ice.

• • • •

Rocky, 1979 – 1983

SHE IS CERTAINLY THE weirdest. As with almost all my relationships, she comes on to me. My sick mind makes ethical exemptions whenever a woman approaches me. Rocky lives right down the hall, in the same adult complex. She parks right across from me in the underground garage. I never dream I'll have a four-year affair with her. She drives a big brown Ford truck, with camper shell. At night, she wears riding clothes and smells of horse. She is very shy, and I am not interested until we talk at that hall party. The adult complex is into singles things. Rocky and I speak for the first time over cups of mulled wine. We see we have something in common. We are both exercise addicts.

Properly raised in Boston fashion, her dad was an electrical engineer who had worked on the Manhattan Project. Rocky works for the pathology department at Kaiser. She is divorced. Her ex is crazy and a drunk. She is a very weird chick. She has her life perfectly structured, down to the minute. She seems to be always in a hurry and worried about something, her job, her horse, her weight. She is anorexic. Only with me, once a week or two, she lets herself go and indulges. Food and sex are what we always do together. She comes alive with me. God am I sick!

I look out her dark bedroom window, to the apartment across the garden courtyard at Jane, who sits on her couch reading, the curtains open. The next night, I'm having sex with Jane, on her couch, with the lights out, the curtain open, looking at Rocky. She sits on her foldaway bed that I shared with her the night before, reading. My life consists of running, eating, and screwing. Work is not a priority.

• • • •

Jane, 1979 - 1983

OF ALL THE ROTTEN THINGS I do to women, the cruelest is to Jane. She shares a two-bedroom apartment with her divorced dad, in my complex. I pick her up. She is just out of college and has a meaningless bank job and dull life. She is slightly plump and horny as hell. We have sex several times every time we get together.

"Teach me everything," she begs me when we make love. I do.

"It's yours," is the last thing she says to me. She grows bitter when I ask if she is sure I'm the father. I take her to dinner to break up when she tells me she is pregnant.

"It's yours, Spence," she says, with deep hurt in her tone. "It's yours."

I pay for the abortion.

• • • •

Mount Diablo

MOUNT DIABLO LOOKS higher than four thousand feet. It stands thirty miles east of San Francisco. Much of California is made up of long running mountains or ridgelines, but Mount Diablo is independent. Because of its great panoramic views, it was used for many years as a survey point and observatory. Before the smog and haze took away visibility, Mount Shasta 300 plus miles to the north could be clearly seen. The ambient night-lights of the surrounding cities and towns make the observatory obsolete.

East of Mount Diablo are the still visible Sierras, the long mountain chain that runs along almost the entire eastern side of California. Mount Diablo is young as mountains go. It is only forty or fifty million years old, young in earth time. Dinosaurs came and went before Mount Diablo popped up. Tectonic plates rub together often in California. Mount Diablo grew that way, pushed straight up out of the ground when plates on the earth's crust collided. It did not suddenly happen. It ground its way upward. Mount Diablo is still growing. The earth is alive. It moves, spews and shakes.

The entire area was once part of an inland sea. Fossilized seashells can be found in the sandy grayish soil on its hillsides. Shell Ridge borders the city of Walnut Creek directly below the northern side of the mountain. White flecks of creatures' past, fossilized remnants of clamshells are imbedded in sandstone. Hills like rounded mounds, landlocked waves, roll into Mount Diablo from the west. Castlerock is a large cluster of unique rock formations on Mount Diablo's western side. Rock spires like bastion walls and castle towers are what gives Castlerock its name. Caves dot the sides of the smooth rock spires.

There are two access roads to the top of the mountain. The most frequent road is from the northern side out of the city of Walnut Creek and the other from its western side. Both access roads converge roughly halfway up, and then continue as a single road to the summit. Castlerock lies below the juncture of these two winding roads. The roads are all paved and wind like snakes along the sides of the mountain. It has become a favorite with bicyclists who endure the vigorous climb of some six miles.

Mount Diablo has magical powers according to the Native American descendants of the area. Their ancestors' basic food source thrived on the sides of the mountain. The bullet like nuts of the black oaks produced their essential starch. They were hunter gatherers, not farmers like their Navajo kin. The black oaks' bark is deeply creased, grayish brown, with tiny leaves of emerald-green, which protects the oaks from the oppressive heat of summer. The acorns after being shelled were soaked in water to leach, then mashed in circular indentations on rocks. Acorns are high in starch content.

After Mount Diablo was "discovered" by the Spanish, they let cattle run wild along its lush, heavily grassed slopes. All they took of the cattle slaughtered were the hides and fat, which they boiled out of the meat for tallow to make candles. Thousands and thousands of cattle were butchered for their leather and fat only. Perhaps the Native Americans ate some of the meat, but most of it recycled naturally by rot and carrion. The Spanish named the mountain after the devil. It does get hot in the summer.

· · · ·

Addictions in Life 1979 Walnut Creek CA

I CANNOT SAY IT IS just this or that. As far gone as I am, I know it is more than one or two things about me that are wrong. It is my lifestyle.

Far back in the wrinkles that hide on the side of Mount Diablo, all alone, I run. Through valleys and canyons that weave and flow up the mountain side. Tinkling streams drip down onto and over smooth rocked stream beds. Small leafed short California oak shade my ascent. I meander up through narrow hidden canyons and over short grassy ridgelines.

Ten miles into a Saturday morning November run I feel secluded. Perfectly in tune with myself, I feel able to run forever. Unafraid. I love that degree of control over myself, from and of myself. Free. Cold new life flows with each breath. Like an an- cient drum beat of a slave galleon my lungs pound out their rhythm. Legs like oars guide me effortlessly over barely touched ground. Cruising, sweatless, in shorts and shoes, no shirt, I run. Forty-two degrees. My skin tingles everywhere.

But this jones cost eighty to ninety hard training miles a week, rain or shine. This is one of the few positives going for me now. Like EST or whatever that spring is, I am hooked. It is the latest godsend for the children of the system. Running. Jogging. Racing. Marathoning. Positive addiction.

It is just a minute shy of eight AM. January. I have been up since four. I stand with two other brain damaged buddies in the damp Stockton cold. Eight hundred other bodies surround me, jumping up and down in anticipation.

I drive eighty miles to run ten. Makes sense to me. In running shoes, socks, shorts and gloves, no shirt, I stand in thirty eight-degree weather.

Count down from ten, then bang! Surging, pushing, I am up in front with the hot dogs. Slapping, squeaking, my rubber soles stream down the smooth asphalt road. Sharp turns wind through new residential areas. Hesitant that first mile, like a horse holding back.

"Six minutes, nine, ten, eleven seconds," I hear as I pass the caller. At five miles I know this will be my best race ever. I am flying. Sixty-two minutes twelve seconds for ten miles. Wonderfully sick afterwards. Elated. Like childbirth.

We watch the football playoffs on a tiny TV while we drive back after the race. From the back seat of the lightly bouncing car, my gaze drifts from TV screen to out the window. Past greens and browns. At peace.

· · · ·

Christopher Columbus 1982

I AM AT THE HEIGHT of my running and other addictions. It is the end to a lazy workout day. I only run six miles at noon. I am resting at Terri's apartment. She is studying to be an attorney. We have a secret affair going for three years. I usually see Terri on Wednesdays. I come straight from work. I sprawl out on a shaggy white couch, one leg hung off the back, vegging to the early evening news on TV, scanning my favorite paper, the San Francisco Chronicle, intermittently.

I want everything to be as predictable as possible. I am a time bomb of rage masking myself with activity. I think running is a positive addiction.

Everything in the Chronicle is as predictable as its green colored sports and business sections. The Chronicle realizes these two groups of readers need the most help. As with many forms of primates, color seems to work best for men.

While I scan the sports section, my lover is preparing pasta, one of my favorite dinners. An outright hot lover, she is an artist with food. Everything is on hold in my life. I am cruising. To hell with my job and my life. I run seventy to eighty miles per week. Sex, eating and running dominate my life.

Columbus Day in San Francisco, an Italian tradition clung to passionately by aging devotees in North Beach, is a dying slice of the Italian part of town. Chinese stores and restaurants intrude on almost every block. Two groups of immigrants fight turf battles the modern way. Money.

The lead for the TV feed is about seeing a genuine-dressed Christopher Columbus land ashore from a small wooden boat. Chris is on one of the last pieces of sand beach in the San Fran- cisco area. In period dress, Columbus wears puffed pants that cling to an aging Italian man's old ass. Just below the knee, cute white lace knee-high socks. Darling, shiny gold little cloth slippers mark his steps ashore. He prances instinctively when dressed and walking like that. He brushes aside a gold cape; a floppy hat with feather trailing marks his skull, covered by a Gloria Swanson type wig. Chris steps ashore. Big smile. Right hand waves from his ruffled sleeve.

The reporter segues to live feed of Chris in the park in North Beach. Drunks and derelicts sit slumped on benches that line its pathways. Christopher stands properly positioned for the well-lit park street shot. Chris has a max grin going. He makes a perfect TV piece for Columbus Day.

"I'm an old man," he says. "I been playin' Christopher Columbus every Columbus Day for over turty yeas," he boasts. This is his day. His town. His turf.

The live TV newsman says with rising glee, "Ladies and gentlemen. Folks back at the studio. Here he is...Mr. Christopher Columbus." The reporters suited arm drapes impulsively over Chris's shoulder. Just as the reporter starts to open his mouth again, a figure lurches onto the screen. The live camera jerks and tracks the intruder.

I drop my paper and say out loud. "Boy, she's a husky sucker." I am wrong. His long black hair fools me. The familiar ragged clothes of a homeless become obvious. He is lurching, fumbling, grabbing. He pounces lightly on Columbus's opposite shoulder.

His hair is held back with a red bandana. "Oh, thank you Maser Columbussss, fer descovering us," the Indian spits his sarcastic dig into Chris's face. Fear fills Chris's eyes. He winces while pulling away from the Indian.

Chris's Italian face shows its seventy plus years. The Native American homeless drunk is sallow-skinned, puffy eyed. His face deeply gorged by street and booze-earned wrinkles is no more than forty. His head rocks slowly in rhythm to his inner drunken song.

The feed cuts back to the studio where the anchors look like they just saw someone crap on camera. The guy anchor says, "Uh, why don't we cut to a commercial message?"

"It is a commercial you asshole!" I scream. "Columbus is a commercial. Johnnie Jack is right."

"Who is right?" Terri asks calmly as she hovers over me.

I say, "Ah to hell with it." As I speak she leans down over me and lifts my chin upward. She firmly cradles my chin with her soft fingers. Wide on my mouth, her kiss lands dead on my lips, silencing me. Her shiny long black hair brushes my eye, my cheek, and my neck. Slowly she finishes her kiss.

Then, in a calm soft demand says: "Come dear, dinner." She pulls me up by my arm. "I want to bathe you after dinner. Then, we'll see what happens," she whispers in my ear as she guides me to my feast.

• • • •

Jimmy Chen, 1983

GRIMACING, HE FINISHES another drag from his ever-present cigarette. Between puffs he jabs skyward, ashes flicking, "Fuck Ray Keene...Fuck Denese Penino," he snarls, smoke hissing out along the sides of his taut lips. One for two. He gets the first right but mispronounces the second man's name. He is committing the ultimate act of debasement for someone of Chinese ancestry. You do not speak the "F" word. Not as a well-behaved Chinese you don't.

Jimmy is a spy sent by headquarters. Everyone sent by head-quarters is a spy. Headquarters is in Hong Kong. The Tung boys own Seapac now. One brother is based in Hong Kong (number one son), the other in N.Y. Daddy Tung fled Shanghai just be- fore the Communists took over. Whatever, however, he is a big shipping tycoon by the early sixties. Old man Tung died re- cently. Seeing and dealing with so many guys like Jimmy makes me wonder how they ever made it. Jimmy is their front-line point man. He is one of their best and brightest. A lot of things he is. Bright? Not a chance. There are times I swear that Jimmy is retarded.

Being in shipping means working for either sales or opera- tions. Ever shifting. Territorial battles. Clashes. Ebbing and flooding, the boundaries of these two monolithic departments change like the tides.

"Fuck sales. Fuck traffic," Jimmy continues. The traffic de- partment often bounces between reporting to sales or operations. Obviously, those in traffic are at odds with we in operations. They work for sales now. All sales does is try their best to give everything away. If it were not for operations watching and attempting to control the costs, we'd lose even more money than we are already losing. That is always the claim of the operations department. Jimmy hates just about everything. Anger fuels anger. It is impossible to stay calm around him. Something is missing from him. As though he is still searching for a soul, a heart. He is heartless, ruthless. Hong Kong loves him. My luck, I work for the idiot. Worst of all he likes me.

• • • •

Real Chinese Food 1984

IT IS THE ONLY TIME I really see them let their hair down. No matter what kind of mood they are in all day, they sit around a big circular table at night and go crazy.

Chow time. Chopsticks click. Loud smacking, chewing. Even the shriveled up, skinny ones go at it. Cigarettes hang out the right side. Talk and laughter comes out the left, and I don't know how, but I swear to God, food goes straight up the middle. All into and out of the very same mouth. Simultaneously. Those suckers talk, laugh, yell, eat, smoke, burp. Chunks of food fly out as they yell or laugh. Duck! Guys look at you and start to talk. This stuff is like crank (amphetamines). Too much MSG.

We always end the evening with a banquet after meetings. This one in New York is especially vicious. Chinese guys from Hong Kong against Chinese guys from New York. I no longer give a damn. Maybe they are acting, screaming at one another that afternoon and evening. At the restaurant they sit shoulder to shoulder eagerly and eat fog.

"What is this?" My chopsticks try to lift what looks like the back of a small bird. Barely poached, white slick flesh, bright red blood veins show.

"Fog," says the Dragon Lady. So much noise I can barely hear her. Chinese restaurant, ten PM. That is serious eating time in Chinatown. They deliberately sit me next to this bitch, knowing we hate each other's guts. I call her Dragon Lady because of her endearing personality.

I have to grab the fog with my fingers, the chopsticks would not hold. Piss on these clowns, I think, chewing. I am starving. The waiters only bring one serving at a time. Weird shit too. No sweet and sour. No chow mein. No rice.

"What did she say this is?" I ask the guy who sits on my other side. It is chewy, almost rubbery. I swallow chunks unchewed.

"Fog," he says. It is late, I am tired, and half shit-faced drunk. He starts to spell it. "F R O G." Ding! The damn thing jumps straight up my throat.

Flash. I start flashing back. That tingle like in Nam comes over me. Those fucking gooks, over and over, flash in my mind. I have to eat their shit too?

"Well, Ernie, what do you think of these Chinese gang- sters?" John asks, smiling brightly. He is the lead clown from headquarters in Hong Kong. He grins and motions with his hand around the table to a grunting ring. Hands with chopsticks dart in and back.

"Well, fortunately I don't understand Chinese, so I don't have to listen to them while I eat." He jerks like a guy who gets hit suddenly. Pale he becomes.

I am still pissed off when we leave the place. Walking out with one of the Americans I ask, "Wonder if that clown understood me?"

"Oh, he read you loud and clear, Ernie. You just committed suicide man."

Asleep that night or early morning, the ultimate nightmare. It seems mid-day. Bright out. I awake, not knowing where I am or what I have done. She is next to me in bed, up on her elbow. Beaming.

Glowing. That fiery look of a woman who's been made love to all night and is ready for breakfast. You.

Oh shit! Please God, I swear I'll change. I'll quit fooling around. I sit straight up. It is still black out. Sweating. Breathing heavy. Heart thumping. It is the Dragon Lady. She has just leaned over to me smiling and says, "After we make love again, I feed you fog."

 • • • •

Outsider 1984

I'M NOT SURE IF IT is a curse, my ability to "stand back" from the situations going on at work. It is both my wisdom and agony. It is like a nagging pain in my back, or tooth, that feeling. After a while it becomes my old friend. I go through all the trips, anger to resignation.

I watch, so detached as people spend all their time at work in games that are pure, unadulterated bullshit. Like a voyeur, I move about the scenes being played, unnoticed. My, my, how I continually set myself up. Why is reassurance such a precious thing?

They preen and prance, dance, and bow, scrape, and grovel for what? A corner office with a view of another building? A coat rack? A card with a meaningless title below their name?

This is my curse. I see "reality." Why do I think that mine is the only view of life? People need their rituals. They seem to rise to their highest level of fear naturally. If they don't have a real crisis, they create one. Work in the transportation business doesn't seem right to the players unless there is a crisis going on. Everyone including me takes turns stirring the pot.

 • • • •

Susan, 1984

DIDN'T SOMEONE ONCE say, "never trust a blind date?" That is how Susan and I meet. Six months before my crash, Oz, a running buddy, sets us up. "A sexy divorcé," is how he describes her. Yes, she is. With her full mouth. Susan has a smile that makes your zipper come down automatically. Oh my, she has such a beautiful smile. She hits me with it hard the first time we meet in San Francisco.

Susan loves San Francisco. She also loves to eat. Susan is the only woman I have been with who could out-eat me. She is not shy around chow at all. She loves dessert, after sex.

It is the Fourth of July in 1984 when we meet. San Francisco blesses us with clear weather. We have Chinese food in Japan town. I guess Susan isn't sure. She knows I am Asian, but not the exact type. That big sexy mouth of hers can process food. This woman has an eating disorder, I think, watching her down the spicy chicken. She's going to excuse herself in a minute and hit the john. I figure she is one of those bulimics or has worms really bad.

She shows her age in her hips only. Susan has a nice figure and pretty legs. She has a mouth that not only displays rare beauty, but a capacity for conversation as well. If Susan isn't putting something into her mouth, it is going the other way, talking. Yak, yak, yak does she love to talk.

I like Susan right away. We hit it off in bed. Passion for food and passion for sex. Susan is an eager, adventurous, uninhibited, full participant. If she has any sexual hang ups, I never see them.

I don't give a shit about anything when I meet Susan. I am about as out of control as you can get. I seek frequent sex as solace for the mess my everyday life has become. My job, investments, running, even sex life, everything is fucked. I've become a metaphor.

We meet six months before I have my breakdown. Though it is never directly discussed, we both know each is seeing and dating others. I am so far out of control I am incapable of having a relationship.

Susan is the only woman I've ever known who could keep up with me. She talks about dieting, but never does. We'd go out for dinner on Friday night, drink wine, pig out on a huge dinner, come home and still nail the ice cream in the freezer. None of this big bowl for me, small bowl for her shit. Sue always takes the larger serving. It has nothing to do with women's lib either. She is just selfish about some things. She is generous as hell with things she doesn't want.

She was raised that way. Breeding. It's mostly about family influence. As the oldest child in a large close family, Sue learned to grab first and eat it before anyone else could. She wasn't poor, far from it.

Living in a wealthy suburb with thrifty parents can make you materialistic and selfish unless your parents explain the need for such thrift. If not, the kids see their peers and start to compare and feel cheated.

Susan married at seventeen to a guy whose family had money. At the time she thought she loved him. They stayed married for fourteen years. By the time we meet she has resolved in her own mind that she really married to get out of her chaotic family home.

She is at a good time in her life when we meet. Ten years single, she has run through the complete list of jerks that life has to offer. By the time I come along she knows what she wants from a man. I am it. She is not shy and often asks me out. We have a wonderful time together. Company, companionship, whatever, it isn't love.

By September of 1984 Susan gets on to my bullshit. I hang up when she rags on me for seeing others. It is okay for her, but not me. She is being a hypocrite.

Funny things happen when I finally have my breakdown. The other women all leave. They are like rats deserting a sinking ship. When I crash, the women who frequent my bed suddenly flee. PTSD frightens them. Fuck me. I no longer have status in society. I quit working. Women take a lot from men, but not from someone with my status, or lack thereof. Sue is the one who reaches out to me. She is not afraid of me. Susan grew up in a dysfunctional family. I fit right in. She finds my insanity fascinating. She loves the fact that I am becoming vulnerable, feminine almost.

Loyalty is one of my magic buttons. Show me loyalty, and I owe you big time. I am in my homeless faze when Susan steps in to help. By the time I have a homeless living in my condo all the other women are gone. Susan makes curtains for my homeless place. She invites me to spend more time with her. I fall into the relationship. It lasts about three months before she goes full blown AIDS. Three months after I move in with her, she gets diagnosed.

Susan and I visit her parents in Fallbrook in Southern California in July of '86. She and her sisters donate blood toward her mother's account. Susan's mother has a hip replacement that requires multiple transfusions. Susan's blood is never used. It takes the blood bank until October to notify her that her blood tested positive for HIV. For all of September her doctor kept misdiagnosing her.

Susan is a blonde from Walnut Creek, she isn't queer. But she slept with one, dangerously, it turns out. She learns of her condition by mail. Her eyes show like a frightened doe caught in the headlights just before impact. I watch her read the fatal mes- sage, her gasp before she flashes the letter at me, which tells her she has AIDS. She sits up, frightened, a shell of her once vivacious self. It says she is HIV positive and should seek medical advice immediately. She is already in the hospital, near death. I feel sorry for her. I promise to stay with her to the end. And I do.

I have Susan to thank for curing me of that dark side of my personality. Watching someone perish before your eyes does change one's perspective. Sex gets put in its place. Susan grows angry with men as she grows weaker, the last year of her life. There is no greater horror than to see someone you sleep with die, slowly. Loyalty is a motherfucker sometimes.

Sometimes I am angry at Susan. She takes out her anger with men on me. She hates her father, but never confronts him. Susan stays as well adjusted as she can by using me and her daughter as recipients of her wrath.

I listen to Susan calmly tell Roger over the phone of her infection and her belief that he infected her. She shows no anger after she hangs up. He denies it all. Susan stays well-adjusted by living her life in the moment, never in the past. She can let go. Susan takes care of herself.

Laurel, a shrink friend, put it succinctly when she says, "You know Ernie, all the bad shit that's happened to your generation, happened to you." Just after Susan dies in 1988, Laurel and I walk a narrow canyon trail in Oakland Park. How true her words. I have indeed had it all.

• • • •

My Muse California 1985

WORDS LIKE HEARTACHE and arduous come to mind when I think of my muse. I walk around sullen during such times. My muse is demanding in her craving for my complete attention.

I go through the motions, while awaiting her. It is as though I am not there, my lover says. My soul is gone. Like some lonely shawl wrapped wife, standing on a high cliff overlooking a storming sea, I wait. Churning and stewing, my feelings raw with anticipation. By now I know the scent of my muse. I am so lonely. It is the worst of times.

I am but a witness, my calling a crime to many. People do not like hearing the truth. Heartlessness is not something one likes to have pointed out. I live in the United States of denial. I am just repeating what my muse says. Honest.

• • • •

Worry

WORRY, WHY DO I LET myself worry? Wondering, what in the world will I do? What is this strange brew we mix for ourselves? So heady it is. Like a man with a problem with drink, we don't seem to know when to quit. On and on it goes.

Oh, I'm so depressed. About what? Life. What is life? Whose life? This is life? Let me see the damn thing once in a while. Try to stop it. How do you stop something you can't really put your finger on?

What you think it is, is really just a symptom. What are the symptoms? Symptoms. Mysterious things those symptoms.

Oh, if I could be like an apple tree. The symptoms rotted fruit. So easy to see. Pick those rotten apples off and toss 'em. Chuck 'em. Throw them out. "Out, out damn spot."

You're not dealing with your problems when they're just symptoms. Sources. You've got to get to the source of your prob- lems, then the symptoms will disappear. When they disappear where do they go? Back in the dark recesses of your mind? Where is your mind? In your head? Ha!

Then why do I feel it in my soul? Soul? You said soul. Oh no! Now we've got to fool with eternity. Eternal worry. I'll never get out of this damn worry.

Not knowing what it is or where to find it, how can I get rid of it? It's not about knowing, is it? Maybe it's about feelings.

Great. Just great. Let's try to put our finger on that one, shall we? If I don't feel worried, am I still worried but just not aware of it at the moment because I'm feeling something else?

Will the worry lie there for years? Dormant, lying in wait to strike. "Gotcha!" it will say, when you least expect it.

It must be tangible since we can share it. We're all so worried about this or that. Is this or that a worry? Who makes it a worry? Who says?

Some people don't worry. Happy go lucky people. Where do they put their worries? Bastards give it to me. These worries can't be mine. They must belong to someone else.

Maybe there's a fixed amount of worry at all times and cer- tain people get more than their share. Get some of this shit off me. I can't stand it. I'm going crazy.

Ah, sweet insanity. Worry free now. Well not really, but at least I've identified the problem. It's "them" not me. If I can just get "them" off me, my worries will disappear.

• • • •

Modern Medicine 1985

I HOPE TO HELL I AM crazy. If not, then society is in big trouble. Thank you, Vietnam. You finally legitimize what people have been feeling for so long. Life sucks.

I learn about myself when I do therapy. My shrink does not tell me what his specialty is. I expect a guy to be Freudian, or whatever. My shrink specializes in not talking. As far as he is concerned, we can go the full fifty minutes without saying a word. His BMW outback is being covered either way.

"What do you want me to talk about?" "Tell me how you feel," he answers.

"If I knew that, what would I need you for?"

"Okay." He sits back further in his chair. Deadpan look.

I think my anxiety is work related. He has me talking Nam inside of three visits. He does it without talking. I wonder if he hypnotizes me.

Since my employer's insurance company is picking up the tab for my therapy, they insist that their own selected shrink examine me too. This is the first time I've ever seen doctors' offices like this. It is like a theater in the round. One receptionist serves thirty doctors. I think they are all psychiatrists. My waiting room is a numbered cubicle forming an inner circle to the building. Doctors' offices form the outer ring.

How symbolic. How tacky. Cubicles hold only cheap plastic chairs. This guy peeks around a corner.

"Spencer. Come with me." Boy, oh boy, I think, this should be fun. I follow a guy who is a slob. He opens the door to his office.

"Wait here. I'll be back in a minute." I am alone in a pigsty. His office is unreal. Under a desk across the small, thinly carpeted room, stacks of files sit piled about. Papers falling out of folders show like fans. Beneath the couch, visible from my low-slung seat are balls of dust like discarded children's playthings.

The insurance company must have put me out for bid. I just love free enterprise. This guy has to be cost effective.

"Wait a minute, can't you see I have to write this all down?" He snaps at me. We have barely started the session. All I've given is my name and date of birth. My autobiography is being done long hand by a licensed psychiatrist. Good luck America. He writes in that tiny little perfect handwriting style that just pisses me off. People like that count out their toilet paper, square by square I bet. I must be in a time warp; tape recorders should have been invented by now, I think.

"Don't you think you married too young?" His half glasses down his nose, he looks over at me, mouth pouting.

"What's too young?" My surprised answer.

"You were only twenty-two, why I didn't marry until my late forties." He seems to puff out saying that. Benchmark established. This clown could not get laid at any club Med. Ever. A mid-fifties, paunchy, thin haired dork. Bet the bride is a real winner I think to myself.

I leave smiling. Both shrinks agree. Work caused my problems. Full disability. God bless America. What did we ever do before modern medicine?

LIFE AFTER VIETNAM - 1986 to PRESENT

Intro

Walnut Creek California

Being a Nam vet is like using Tabasco on everything. It has its own special flavor. Last time I saw him we posed for a photo together. He probably doesn't remember me. Why am I doing this? After all these years? I punch in the numbers. It rings into my past.

"Hello," Ken's voice passes into my ear. "May I speak to Ken Pipes please?"

"Ernie Spencer? Is this the Spence? Hey, are you still in Hawaii?"

"How did you recognize my voice after all these years?" "Goddamn Spence, your voice is exactly the same. The hair on the back of my neck is standing straight up."

Eighteen years melt away. It has been this long since we fought side by side. Getting hammered and I don't mean booze. I feel as though we had never been apart. A writer doing a history on the battle of Khe Sahn gave me Ken's phone number. From Ken comes the names and numbers of others who I had served with. In the next week I call and speak with Chaplain Stubbe, Harvey the doc, J.B. our commanding officer.

Most of all I call and visit Ken. We were very close. True in Nam, brothers in the deepest sense. While I get out of the Marines right after Nam, Ken stays in for twenty-four years. He retires from the Marine Corps, a lieutenant colonel.

Now he works at a nuclear power plant in security. Ex-Marines make good guards. Real good paper pushers too. Ken pushes paper for a security detachment. He hates the "plant."

Welcome to Vietnam, Macho Man is out in manuscript. My family and friends think it's a knockout story and want me to publish it. I'm in a monogamous relationship. Who could have ever imagined it would have happened this way?

. . . .

Delta House Oakland CA 1986

Swallowing the Bait

DELTA HOUSE STARTS from therapy. It is as though some mysterious hand moves, guides me towards what is to come. Most of what my shrink and I talk about concerns Vietnam. I'm the first combat induced post-traumatic stress disorder case this shrink ever does. I am a newfound jewel, what he had only read about, pondered abstractly, before having me.

Feelings. My problem is feelings, or lack thereof. I guess I shut it down a little too far in Nam. Weird. I came home and worked and all. You can't read about feelings, you've got to ex- perience them, live. I start writing about Vietnam. The stuff I'd relive at home is so "real." Feels real.

"The feelings happened," he says, deep the intensity of his look. He admits that he is fascinated by my condition. "I look forward to our visits," he confides.

Sun lights the particles of lint, suspended in the glow of its full, bright yellow afternoon rays. Curtains of dull white muslin billow inward, a gentle breeze through the open windows. The right corner of his cheek and chin catch the sunlight that shines like a spotlight angled downward.

Again, he speaks. "You don't know how much worthless talk I listen to in this job. Some of the people I see don't have a thing wrong with them other than boredom. This is good stuff." His eyes intent, shadowed, unsmiling, his head nods in agreement to his words.

Great. At least I'm not boring. Sick is sick, however; psychic wounds are psychic wounds. He knows psychiatry, I guess. Door after door seems to open. Emotions come pouring, screaming out of me.

After a while, I want to confront Vietnam again. I want to know if it is just me who feels these feelings. I read about it. This is supposed to be a common thing with not only Vietnam, but all combat vets. I like seeing for myself.

Psychiatrists are not supposed to act disappointed, but mine is. I tell him I want to try group therapy. He does not do groups. After fifteen months of private therapy, I am ready to listen to someone else's shit, not just mine. Is this sharing?

* * * *

The Road to Delta

MY SHRINK SETS ME UP with another shrink who runs a Vietnam veterans rap group in Berkeley. Where better to be loony than in Berkeley, I laugh to myself as I drive to my first group meeting. It's a cold Tuesday night in March at a place called the Veterans Assistance Center.

"Enter at your own risk," a yellow sign on the large wooden door at the entrance warns me. This had been a grammar school before it was condemned by the state for building and earthquake code violations. This poor section of Berkeley has the Hayward fault running through it.

The laughter and playful shouts of children now gone. In their place disheveled, tired veterans with vacant eyes shuffle about.

Boy I bet the brothers who come here high on whatever, trip out on this place being officially condemned. They must flash right back to Nam. Do not pass go.

Symbolism is cruel. What does this shit mean, I ask myself? I shouldn't deal with this? Typical Uncle Sam bullshit again, playing with us. We can't even meet unless it's under risky conditions. Beautiful.

I walk through a couple of swinging doors and into a small well-lit room. In its center is a large folding table around which sit raunchy guys fresh off the street. They seem like a raggedy, dried out, flower lei. Garlands grown parched and faded. Faces wind-burnt from living outdoors. Tussled hair, eyes deep-set, follow me in. I watch brittle skin, ready to crack faces, and bloodshot eyes seat me. "Welcome," the dorky, skinny, oldest guy says.

Feeling like I just arrived home after a long journey, a surge of awareness, belonging, fills me. These guys stink. Why is it, no matter what other odors, piss is always a part?

Tattered, matted hair, hunched in their chairs, Nam guys. That ole feeling of Nam tingles in me for the first time in almost nineteen years. You been gone a long time Ernest, my inner voice says to me as my eyes scan the room once again.

• • • •

Rap Group Therapy

HOW REFRESHING IT IS to not feel out of place. I am with kindred souls. Anger expressed flows like wine at a wedding, during the rap meetings. Hard lives lived fly around the room. The realization that the world does not understand us rings out loudly. No holds, (except violence) let it out. Everyone dumps out their fears and frustrations. From this crew of societal misfits, I learn. Nam was just Nam. If you play, you pay. Tough shit Ernest, it just happened. Nam happened, fact.

After a few sessions I realize how easy I really have it. I am driving a new four-wheel drive big snow tires Blazer, while these guys sleep on the streets. I'm skiing up in the mountains at Tahoe while these guys try to scrounge a meal.

My Catholic conscience cannot handle this realization. Those Catholic nuns are going to haunt me to the grave, I swear. "We must always help the poor. The poor are God's children," they'd say. I take one guy home for a "few days."

Impulsively, one night after rap I ask if he'd like a shower and a roof.

· · · ·

John

HE HAD BEEN IN THE Navy and in Nam. Detroit was his hometown. With his background came poverty, a white alcoholic father and sexual abuse as a child. You can change your attitude about judging others when you see them in a more personal context.

John had struggled to get ahead. That's why he joined the Navy. John believed electronics was his ticket out of poverty. The Navy kept its promise. He got the electronics training. He never made anything of it after Nam. Neither college, marriage and child, or East Indian mysticism seemed to do it for him.

Despite being an electronics technician with almost a college degree, the streets and homelessness wear heavy on John. He is tiny, almost frail. I feel sorry for him.

John talks rationally but he is always way inside. A loner. He looks bat-shit crazy sometimes. He usually behaves like a little angel. John is mentally ill and does not realize it. In his mind it is the rest of the world that is fucked up. It is "they," never him and his beliefs.

"We gonna dig up Lyndon Johnson's bones and straighten his ass out about Vietnam, huh John?" I mock him one night.

I care for him. Feed him, give him my clothes. Guilt is something isn't it? My feelings of guilt motivate me. Thank you sister whatever your name was. No stupid man is John. Many an evening we sit, late into the night, talking. The depletion of the earth's resources is a major concern of his. On matters outside himself John seems fine. Whenever he enters the equation however, his sickness shows. With the eyes and expression like Charles Manson, he vents his hatred of the "system."

Conspiracies everywhere lurk in the minds of people so ob- sessed. John is trapped in madness.

"He is blind to himself, he has a big problem," I tell myself. But, if he's got big glaring problems and can't see them, what does that mean? Could I be out of control too and not realize it?

John's tiny stature matches his ambition, pack rat. Jesus, he scrounges the slinkiest junk you could imagine. His ambition is to work in the secondhand business full time. I think the most worthless piece of junk he brings home is the broken, I mean smashed up, old wooden player piano. It looks like it threw-up on itself. Keys, wires, things spray out from the cracked, sagging

frame of what was once a nondescript cheap piano.

"This will be worth a fortune after I fix it up," his impish, bearded leprechaun face and smile so bright, assure me. I loan John the money to get into the garage sale business. He plans to go to garage sales on weekends, find bargains and sell the merchandise during the week to people who work the flea markets as vendors. John's plan is illusive. Almost all the shit gets stored at my small condo, out on the back porch. He never sells anything to anyone, but he does buy mounds of junk.

• • • •

Mark

MARK IS IN OUR RAP group and also lives on the street. He is ex-Army infantry, Nam vet, white, alcoholic, and gay. John and I visit Mark at the Menlo Park VA hospital after he turns himself in for the second time in less than a year. Mark has been unsuccessful in past attempts at completing the VA treatment program for post-traumatic stress disorder.

Menlo Park Veterans Administration hospital is south of San Francisco, near San Jose. Handling primarily Vietnam era veterans, the hospital provides treatment and counseling for veterans with addiction or post-traumatic stress disorder problems. Typical treatment consists of voluntary confinement for periods of from three to nine months with intensive psychotherapy as the primary treatment. Mark lasts less than two months.

"I left because I just wasn't ready to deal with the hard stuff about Nam yet," he says. So, he moves into my small condo. Mark is mostly bullshit. I'm no therapist, but I'd say it is due to his denial. The bullshit I mean. His reality must be so painful that he has to deny everything, ego bullshit. Mark lies even when he doesn't have to. Example: At rap you can say anything and not raise an eyebrow. There is nothing you could have done that shocks the brothers at rap. Between them they had eaten, beaten, or screwed everything imaginable. But don't lie at a rap group. The brothers do not like lying bullshitters at rap. Mark is the exception. He is so full of shit the guys laugh him off.

"When was the last time you had a drink, Mark," the shrink asks at the meeting.

"Two weeks," Mark deadpans. His cheeks are flushed red from the half pint of vodka he just chugged down minutes earlier. Bob nods towards me, our eyes meet, a tiny grin breaks across the kinky stubble of beard on his black face. His sad, dark eyes give off a tinkle, a twinkle, a glint of light to match his grin. Bullshit recognition.

Mark reminds me of a small boy. His mannerisms, the vibes he gives off, everything except his looks seem young. The crow's feet on his face, the heavy lines around his eyes, they speak his age, but he is young. Mark never grew up. Shit. Did you have your act together when you were eighteen? That's how old Mark was when he got his bell rung in Vietnam. Mark always has a buzz on and drunk at rap. During rap he comes alive when reliv- ing his firefights.

The doctor "invites" Mark to come to a meeting sober and relive his experiences. Doc says you aren't dealing with your problems when you're high.

"You are dealing with the drug not the problem," doc says. Doc is talking medicine. Mark is talking reality. Fact. Booze or drugs lets the Nam guys at least "seem" to feel. At least that's what a lot of Nam vets "feel." They call the trip self-medication.

. . . .

Delta House

MY CONDO IS TOO SMALL. I want to help more guys. I find a great huge old house in Oakland. I know the rent will be cheap. It is boarded up. As I'm looking it over the guy repainting it says to me,

"Buddy you have got to be out of your fucking mind if you move here. This was the neighborhood crack house. You ain't black, they'll kill you." The owner is a slum lord. He likes my idea of moving in a bunch of homeless vets so much he gives me the place rent free. He even buys the materials to fix it up.

. . . .

Biledow

MARK DOESN'T GRACEFULLY walk out of the closet about his being gay. Biledow pulls it out of him. Biledow is, like Mark, Army infantry Vietnam. Like Mark, alcohol is his primary drug. I believe Biledow wants to die. Every time he gets drunk he tries to piss people off enough to kill him.

"Why don't you have the guts to kill yourself you fucking redneck?" It is at a rap session at Delta House. I am just back from my winter cabin in Tahoe when I scream that at Biledow. Earlier in the session, Mark starts that thread of thought.

"I can fucking kill you, you son of a bitch. Don't you fucking realize that?" Mark says, standing over Biledow who sits on a couch. Biledow has been calling Mark a fag queen for several days. None of the other guys interferes.

Passive we sit, watching. Mark glaring, snarling; Biledow, a small smirk on his calm face looks like a Christian at peace beneath the roaring, hungry lion. When Mark calms down, he sits. As though he has been playing some part, the make-up and role of his earlier straight self dissolves before us. With eyes of disgust, darting, flashing at us, Mark speaks,

"I've always been gay." He seems dignified, we intrusive. As things will be among the insane, Mark and Biledow become friends, drinking buddies, lovers. One night, Biledow tries to piss someone off at rap. Mark jumps up, prances over to him, sits on his lap and says: "Honey let's go fuck and end this nastiness." Then, he runs his fingers through Biledow's hair.

There are two bedrooms upstairs, three downstairs and two living rooms, two baths and a large alcove off the kitchen at the rear of the house. The basement has been made into another apartment. Louvenia lives there.

John, white Bob, Mark, Biledow and David are the original residents. Guess who is the first to go? Right, dear brother John who immediately picks fights with everyone. He is lucky no one kills his ass. I let the house decide with John.

Learning as I go, I choose democracy. Cold-blooded, ruthless democracy. Majority rules in Delta House. I only rule if I have to.

"Don't make me judge you, brothers," I tell them that night. Less than two days after Delta House opens we have our first "showdown." John's 2 AM call demands it. People are staking out territory. John feels threatened. At the meeting he makes the most outlandish demands.

"I will not live here unless I'm treated in a positive manner," John's insane eyes haunt the room.

"Fuck you, who the fuck do you think you are mother- fucker," white Bob snarls back at him.

John tries part time living at the house after that. He keeps his room and his junk in a small back room.

"Ernie, this is Bob." His deep black resonate voice billows into my ear through the phone. By now black Bob has moved in. "That crazy motherfucker John done dragged a stray dog home. He washed the fucking dog in our bathtub. You gotta talk to that crazy fool before one of the guys kill him."

When I get there an hour later John is gone. I wait for him. Little sneaky fucker knows I'm coming and splits. But I wait. Shortly after dawn John comes back. The mutt is blackish with grey throughout. It's skinny, long bodied, ribs showing, with a long tail that seems to be stiffening. One eye is opaque, the other dark.

"I think he might be part wolf that's why his one eye is almost bluish." John tries to ease me into a gentle conversation. We sit out back on the rickety, wooden porch steps. He strokes the dog between its ears. "What do you think, Ernie? He picked me out. He'll die if we just turn him into the pound. I know the guys don't want any pets in the house, but I just feel so sorry for him. What would you do Ernie?"

"Shoot the fucking dog, John." I stand, turn, and walk away. John moves out, slowly. He tries to come back several weeks later. No room. You only get one chance at Delta House.

• • • •

Double Raps

THE SHRINKS AT THE Berkeley rap group also run one in Richmond on Thursday nights. They think I provide a positive image to the vets and ask that I also attend the Richmond group. Being like a kid with a new toy, I accept. Richmond is one of the poorest black communities in the Bay Area. I'm being redundant aren't I? Most of the vets who come to the Richmond rap stay at least part time at the Richmond Rescue Mission. More about that later.

Richmond is a man's hangout. Not of the country club variety, however. Unlike my hometown of Walnut Creek, where one hangs out at the tennis court, pool, or golf club, Richmond dudes use the sidewalk.

"Everythin goes by hea's gotta get by this mothafucker," the old black wino says swaying, staking out his turf. He's up against the paint peeling, windows boarded, stucco building. The ever present small brown bag clutched with rounded hand, the winos tool for passing time. Richmond dudes cluster on sidewalks, jiving, drinking, drugging, and bullshitting. Golfers use a putter; both types of guys are the same, just hanging out, killing time, bullshitting their way through life. One admired, one despised, both for doing the same thing.

Those shrinks talk me into driving the guys staying at the Richmond Rescue Mission to and from rap.

"Pappi, why does your car always smell like old barf and piss?" My daughter grills me. How could I tell her that it was Jesus? Swear to Christ. He is the one who stunk up my car.

• • • •

Jesus

IT'S PRONOUNCED HAY-Zeus, like calling that big time Greek god. He likes to be called Tony, but his real name is Jesus. Jesus was a doggie (US Army) in Nam. Mexican dude. Think of what your stereotypical street bum, wino, almost completely gone character would look like, that's Jesus. When he talks it is like you have to wait for the slot machine to go a spin between words.

"Ca-ca-can," clunk, clunk goes the handle, wheels of fruit in his head spinning as his eyes flutter. "Yo-oou," clunk, clunk, "give me money," clunk, clunk, "fo-ooa cigarettes?" A professional full-time wino and panhandler, Jesus always hits me up for money. It is his job. The reason he talks slow and walks like he's just come ashore after three years in a small boat, is because he got hit in the head. Jesus was Army infantry, airborne, helicop- ters, while in Nam. Word is that he walked into the tail rotor blade of a chopper during a hot landing. Whatever, he seems almost retarded. It's because he can't talk and walks real funny and waddles, but he understands.

I have a real sarcastic way of telling stories. It takes a certain amount of intelligence to follow me. I'm doing a long one that night at rap and Jesus is grinning and grooving right along. Jesus looks into me as our eyes meet while I scan the audience of eyes. Wide is his grin, alive and focused his usually drifting eyes.

It is the shrink who taunts us to take Jesus into the house. I am against it. We don't have the ability to take care of him. Jesus needs full time treatment. He has been in and out of VA hospitals since Nam. Every couple of weeks the Richmond police arrest him so he can spend a few days in the psychiatric ward drying out.

Jesus lasts three days at Delta house. Boy does he look good. The guys bathe him and cut his hair. He wants his long beard shaved off. He looks just like one of the guys, just moderately fucked up looking. The house is in Oakland. Jesus only knows Richmond. He can't panhandle enough in the new environment and so he splits. Jesus needs booze more than a home. It is just his reality.

· · · ·

Rescue Me

LIKE THE CLOSEST THING to Mecca, the Richmond Rescue Mission is all that and more. If you live on the streets in the vicinity of Richmond, California, it is Mecca. Its unpretentious outside belies the wonders within. In the heart of the ghetto, the Richmond Rescue Mission is good ole I believe in JEEEE-ZZUS!

With an organization that would put any corporation to shame, the Richmond Rescue Mission provides food and shelter for the needy. No questions asked. You will notice I did not say free. You get fed three times a day at the mission, after mandatory attendance at prayer meeting.

The Mission's god is not of the mellow variety. God does love us. Why else would he send his son and let the evil in us kill him. The Lord is tired of us bullshitting and the word is that you best get it together. Bible thumping, scream and shout at chapel three times a day every day, that's what you get for free.

It shocks me to see this unpretentious looking white guy running the place. I am there to "deal" with the Reverend Lee. I envision him being this big blow hard black dude. I am the fool, stereotyping again. Since I am paying for everything, I hope to get food and furniture from the Mission as cheap as possible. Most of the guys who move into my place come from there. The two Bobs, David, and Jesus all live at least part time at the Richmond Rescue Mission. When the Reverend listens to my plan he refuses any payment and instructs his staff to give me food and furniture for our place. Another myth of mine debunked. Like a pie in my face, the anti-religious bias of mine gets it square on target. In all my dealings with the homeless it is without exception the "Christian" variety of groups who are most involved. Come to think of it, that is the essence of Christ's message. The Reverend Lee educates me. He seems religiously "narrow minded" and yet he is doing this. He is walking the walk and not just talking it.

The mission can sleep forty men in one large dorm. Twelve women are sheltered in another. The maximum stay is seven days. You can go beyond seven days and even move into progressively nicer quarters, If you play the game.

"It takes us about eighteen months to stabilize a homeless man for the Lord." As we slowly walk the spotlessly clean corridors, the Reverend Lee gives his running narrative. "After a man stays seven days, he is given a chance to go on probation for another thirty. He's required to not only attend services but also work the premises. This group provides the bulk of our work force here." We wind our way to the top floors of the maze of interconnected buildings.

"And here are the disciple's quarters," with a sweep of his hand his words play across the inner sanctum of Mecca. These disciples are way into God. They run the work crews but spend most of their time studying the bible. After thirty-seven days, if you keep your shit together, you too could have this. A disciple for the Lord you'd be. Besides three squares a day, an upper or lower bunk in a clean more spacious dorm than the street people get. As a disciple you also get paid fifteen dollars a month.

Families are also housed in small single rooms until they receive assistance in finding permanent housing or go on welfare. Families are given thirty days room and board free, and chapel services three times a day. Amen!

"And this is the core of our operation," the reverend's words ring out. Into a cold spacious clean computer room we walk. Machines are whirring, singing, pleading for the Lord. "We obtain the bulk of our operating income this way, and believe me, this operation costs money." More a businessman than a minister of the Lord, I now understand the success of the mission. The Reverend Lee is a slick operator. "This computer is tied into various lists of Christian groups that are sensitive to our cause. Our computers do mass mailers every week. We try to cycle everyone at least once a month." If you are on one of his lists you get hit up twelve times a year, minimum. The direct marketing approach not only produces cash, but food, clothing, and furniture.

The reverend likes me. I get free food and furniture for the home. No, I don't have to attend chapel either. Amen!

· · · ·

Brother David

DAVID IS THE ONLY ONE I specifically want for Delta House. He is a brother Marine, combat vet.

"What did you do in Vietnam?"

"I was a rifleman." The long lashes to his droopy eyes hang out there as he answers the shrink's question.

No further summation need be given. If you were a Marine rifleman in Vietnam people needn't ask where you were stationed or what you did. You were stationed in deep shit. The Marine Corps always sent their riflemen into nasty shit in Nam. You could bank on it.

David loves alcohol. Family tradition. His dad also loved alcohol. His dad was also a veteran. During World War II the services were segregated. David's dad being black served in the Army.

David loves to stomp around the house when he gets drunk. He is a fair skinned, good looking black man with droopy, dreamy eyes, and a bald shaved head.

Louvenia, who lives downstairs in the basement calls me at all hours of the night about David. It is the people at the house who give her my number. I call the house right back.

"Put David on the phone now," I say. I get real nasty at three in the morning.

"Hello." His voice is as droopy as his look. "You drunk again brother?" I snap.

"Nah man." His response slow, unconvincing.

"Then why in the hell is Louvenia calling me about you?"

"Ah man Ernie, she just wants to fuck me is all. I won't fuck her, and she's pissed off. I'm cool, Ernie."

Brothers are beautiful aren't they? How can you hate a guy who bullshits so beautifully? Blame a woman. Ultimate denial.

I made the people at Delta House let David stay until he got into a psychiatric ward at Menlo Park. He stays over three months at the VA facility. He keeps asking me to come and meet with his shrink.

Cindy runs the house after a while. She has a Coast Guard past and her own problems with crack cocaine, but Cindy does manage to see that the assigned tasks are carried out. I pay her to do the cooking. I am being sexist, I know.

• • • •

My Brother Ken - Fallbrook, CA 1987

HURLED BACK TO THE world. Three months after me. To Fallbrook, California where he and I now nineteen plus years later speak.

In a dark almost bunker-like living room of his house we sit talking for hour upon end. The Marine Corps everywhere. Case of medals, bookshelves exclusively military in content. Ashtrays, paperweights, and pictures of Marines. Everything marked with a Marine Corps emblem. A lieutenant colonel of marines in full dress blues, chest full of medals, his lady by his side. Ken and Sharon, a picture on the wall.

Ken tells me his story: Yeah, Ernie, I got back in September of 1968. Sharon and the two boys waited for me here in Fallbrook while I was in Nam with you. After all the shit we go through in Nam, after all that I get 'I and I' duty. Inspector and Instructor. I'm the casualties reporting officer for Northern Los Angeles county. You remember how many Mexicans we had fighting as line Marines? You remember how many died with us? You have any idea how many Mexicans there are in that district I covered? For the next three years after Nam, I bury Marines killed in Nam.

First Sergeant would open that little sliding window that separated his office from mine. He'd hold out his phone, that look in his eye, say it was Washington. A migraine in a knife thrust would hit my skull.

Boom! Not until they folded the flag from his coffin, and I handed that flag to his mother or wife would the headache leave me. Sometimes I had several going at once. First Sergeant was a Mexican. After every funeral we'd go to a Mexican bar in the San Fernando Valley. Mexican dude owned the place. Ex-Marine. He would never let us pay.

"Captain, you bury our brother Marines, the least I can do is let you drink my tequila and beer. Never pay me my friend."

Ken continues: Ernie, that's the closest I ever came to being an alcoholic. Like I told Sharon, 'Honey,' I said, 'if that tour of I and I duty didn't make me a drunk, nothing ever will.' Just our luck, huh Ernie? Maybe some of us are meant to be dumped on. Hell, I don't know. During peacetime I and I duty is a dream job. You're an Inspector and Instructor to Marine Reserve Units. You are supposed to go around and check up on reserve units based in your area. But if you had my territory when I did from 1968 through 1971 you spent almost all your time making casualty calls. As you know Ernie, the Marines always have an officer personally inform the family of any wounded, seriously ill, or killed in action Marine.

I was beat in my blues by brothers of one dead Mexican Marine. They beat me on their porch as I came to their door, even before I said a word. They knew instinctively that their brother was dead. Before anyone could tell them, they knew. I'm sorry your brother died, I say. They cursed the Marine Corps and spat on me.

I walked in on one young wife of another dead Marine, and she was on the couch with a guy. Right there in the living room. Through the open screen door, I see them. She asks me when she'll get the insurance policy payment. As soon as I tell her that her husband's been killed that's the only thing she wanted to know. Not when or how he died. I had it all memorized, but she didn't give a shit. Just the ten thousand. That's all she wanted, the money.

I almost felt good about doing the wounded calls. I'd jump on 'em when they saw me. Your son's going to be fine I'd almost yell at 'em.

But I think the worst one I ever did was that old couple. He was their sole surviving son, which would have permitted him to skip service in Nam. But he wanted to be a Marine his father said, and just after he said that the old man had a heart attack. The chaplain and I did everything we could before the ambulance arrived. Man, oh man, Ernie, imagine that poor old lady having to bury her son and husband like that. That was the worst. I buried forty-five Marines on that tour.

My next wasn't bad. Being an instructor at the Command and Staff College in Virginia. Then I did tours at Pendleton here near Fallbrook, Okinawa, then recruiting duty.

My last tour, Ernie, my last duty station was recruiting. I was responsible for the six Western states. Hell, before I could even cover my territory I get a bad fitness report. My territory didn't make its recruiting quota. Complete unsatisfactory marks all the way down my record. Some colonel above me who's trying to make general tries to screw me over. Ernie, that useless son of a bitch isn't fit to carry either of our ruck sacks. That guy was a paper pusher his entire Marine career.

I resigned from the Marine Corps. I got out with my twenty- four years and a pension. Life's never what you thought it would be is it?

I wanted to be a Marine. Into battle with them we went, and they died. I bury them for the Corps. And at the end some prick says I can't get enough fresh Marines for Corps.

"Jesus Christ, Babe," I say as I lean over on the couch and hug him close to me. "Mine's been a piece of cake compared to yours."

. . . .

How a Marine Turned Into A Protester 1987

**From a family of soldiers to Vietnam,
to the peace vigil at Concord Naval Weapons Station**
This article was published in the San Jose Mercury News, Sunday morning, October 4, 1987.

I REMEMBER LOOKING at a family photo a while back. I was maybe six at the time. Around me cousins sat grinning and behind us stood serious aunts and uncles. Every man in that picture had served in the U.S. armed forces. The uncles fought in the good war, World War II, and we boys in Vietnam. That's who we are, we Spencers. Patriots. Not "lifers," just ordinary citizen soldiers.

Vietnam taught me what I wanted in life. I had joined the Marines to be accepted by my country—all my heroes were warriors. But serving at Khe Sanh during the Tet offensive changed my point of view. After that, all I wanted was peace.

For the next 17 years the desire proved elusive. As a shipping industry executive I fought a non-lethal but spiritually repellant battle every day. We had to win business. The other company or the other salesman had to lose. We were bent on destroying each other. Somehow "the world" (that dreamland we had called everything outside Vietnam) failed to provide the inner sense of peace I had so longed for.

Post-traumatic stress disorder floored me a couple of years ago. I had "bunkered" myself way in during my tour in Vietnam. I had thought "Who cares? I'm out now." But PTSD and therapy opened me up. In rap groups, I found other vets who shared my desire for peace, many of whom lived on the streets. America's very own MIAs.

I took a homeless veteran to my house and somehow ended up opening a shelter for veterans. More than 20 vets were fed, clothed, and housed in that year. I was able to keep the home open. Maybe I wasn't patient enough, but I never got any help from the system. I went to the Veterans Administration, county governments, mental health agencies, and the vets problems proved too much for me to handle alone. All of the vets were substance abusers.

But in the midst of madness I had found some peace. I was finally addressing my guilt feelings about the war. As much as helping them, I was helping myself find a way to live.

What's happening now in America is a flashback for Vietnam vets. The crew cuts of the young, the rhetoric about having to stop communism before neighboring countries fall, are all "samey same" as we used to say.

We see it again in photographs of those poor, poor people in Central America. Their skin is brown instead of yellow, but the look in their eyes is no different from what we saw among Vietnamese peasants. Repetitive terror creates that look. We didn't mean to terrorize those people, but they were in the way. The commies were hard to find, but the innocent were everywhere. There was nowhere for them to go, they were home.

The worst-case scenario happened in Vietnam. It went communist, repressively communist. But it's not remotely a threat to the U.S. government. It was their revolution, their business, we vets now realize. Our America withdrew to lick its wounds, but now the country seems to be itching for another fight.

Watching the Iran-Contra hearings I noticed Ollie's look. When he would pause and let his guard down for a moment, I could see that look of fear on him. Fear. Poor Ollie, still hoping to win one big, hoping to end his fear.

Day after day, I am out at the Concord Naval Weapons Station. My sign, "Veterans for Peace," stirs hostility. A thumb down or a finger up seems so undignified from a senior citizen.

I won't stop the weapons from killing those dear brothers and sisters in Central America. My brother Marines stand guard behind fences and barbed wire ensuring the movement of those bombs and rockets. I see myself in them.

Most of the Marines guarding against me are just out of high school on their first tour of duty. Though they were ordered not to talk to us, Marines are Marines—curious. They're bewildered to see so many veterans out there.

"Tell me son," I asked one, "Did you think when you joined the Marines that you'd have to stand behind barbed wire against your fellow citizens?"

"No (expletive) way," he responded.

I'm sorry to offend my neighbors and cause them such distress. But I did my time on the line, folks, for you. I deserve my sense of peace. I am at peace there, at Concord, hurting no one.

My oldest nephew just entered West Point. My dad thinks our policy in Central America is right.

"If we don't stop them there, sooner or later they'll be at our door," he says.

Don't worry America, the Spencers will continue to defend you. I love my family, but I think I've had enough violence. This old Marine needs his peace of mind, which I find out there at Concord. There's nowhere for me to run; I live here. I guess I'm selfish.

• • • •

Telling My Parents the Bad News 1988

IT BOTHERS ME NOT TELLING my parents that I'm going to Nicaragua. They find out from my daughter, Evie. She thought they knew. It is their fiftieth wedding anniversary.

Overlooking the Oakland estuary with sailboats docked all about us, we laugh to singing waiters. They carry a cake with candles flickering. Stopping before my embarrassed mother the waiters surround her and sing to bright smiles on mom and dad.

I'm going with a group from Marin County. They're going to build a school near Condega, in Contra country. At least the Contras think so. They recently shot up and mortared the farming co-op where the school will be located. Contras have not gotten around to fighting the Sandinista army yet. They're still practicing on the civilians.

Mom and dad are so loving, cute, holding hands, kissing tenderly. I just don't want them worrying about me.

My plan is to tell them just before I leave. That way they will spend less time worrying. I guarantee you I'm now number one on their list of worries. That's one trait of mine I attribute more to my parents than anyone else. We can worry with the best. Perhaps this type of worrying is grounded in the Great Depression. The Depression profoundly affected my parents, especially mom. Her family went from having to not having during the Depression.

Mom used to make me eat foods I didn't like by telling me that the kids in China were starving.

"Here mom send them mine," I said to her one evening. I wasn't a big meat eater as a kid, but I did it for the kid in China who didn't have any. During the late forties it was the Chinese who played the part now played by the Central Americans. The oppressed.

"Mom how is my eating this really going to help them?" My cocky, logical mind the propagator, my grin certain, smugly I await her surrender.

She gives me the supreme mother's answer.

"Because I said so," she gently nods. Actually it was not a bad piece of meat and she must have been right. China is doing a lot better.

Speaking of the Depression, that's another thing about my parents' generation; they get to put a lot of THEs before their events. THE Depression, THE War, THE answers.

We're never late, we Spencers. You can bank on it. That's another side benefit of the worrier, punctuality.

"We'll be late if we don't get going," mom would say in a startled voice. It matters not that the trip will take only twenty minutes and reservations are not for another two hours. Sometimes we'd burn ourselves out worrying about an upcoming event.

You can learn to spot worriers. Look for the clocks in their homes. When you see one in the bathroom you know you've found one.

Am I afraid about going to Nicaragua? Somewhat. But at least in Nicaragua the government and especially its military are trying to protect the population. The opposite situation exists in most of the other Central American countries.

"It's ready to explode down there," Duncan, my friend who just returned from El Salvador, tells me. With the eyes of one who has just been with violence, Duncan seems so distraught. He witnessed the relocation of Salvadoran refugees from Honduras back to El Salvador. Americans and other citizens from around the world are, like Duncan, using their bodies to protect the Salvadorans from their military. El Salvador's military, like our Contras, are U.S. supplied and trained. Freedom Fighters, Reagan calls them. Don't make me puke. Why can't we be on the side of the people for once? Why are we always backing the thugs and goons?

The threat of violence is more a drudgery to me than a panic attack. One of the benefits of being a Vietnam vet, I guess. I just do not feel bad about this trip. I'm wide open emotionally.

I heard a beautiful woman speak last night. Carmen is her name. Donna Carmen is a Salvadoran, Quaker, and teacher of special education. She just spent the last year in Nicaragua teaching children and their teachers. We met at a party in Berkeley held in honor of her return. Carmen cannot go back to her country of El Salvador. She is a threat to certain people. They have the guns, supplied by us. They call the shots in Carmen's life, at least in her country. Her crime I guess is being a teacher.

"My government in Salvador is a puppet of the military. It is the same in Honduras and Guatemala." Anger shows as she speaks. "Nicaragua's greatest lesson is that it teaches you humility." The tone of her voice adjusts. As only a teacher can, she speaks words balanced with just the right inflection and expression. Her eyes are dark, showing her native roots. Soft gray hair falls over her tanned face. Her smile is clean.

She enthralls me for over an hour. The good and bad about Nicaragua she tells, pulling no punches.

"I am amazed that the people are still alive." Her inflection rises. "There is nothing there. Even if you have the money there is nothing to buy. You are strangling them. The U.S. economic embargo of Nicaragua is working. But it's the children who are suffering the most, not the communists." After a momentary pause, she continues. "There is corruption and graft. There is bad alcoholism. But it is a beautiful revolution." Finishing these words her lips part over an onrushing smile. "You can see it and feel it in the people."

Then just as suddenly the smile turns to panic. "My God why, I cannot understand Why are you doing this to them? The revolution must succeed in Nicaragua. I am Salvadoran, but if we do not help the Nicaraguans, then there will never be a chance for the other people in Central America to be free. Must America only equate democracy with capitalism?" Ending her plea, a soft plaintive smile again appears.

I'm going to Nicaragua because it just feels like now is the right time. Have you ever felt that way? You just know deep down inside it is time to do something. That's why I'm going, no other reason. Sorry mom and dad.

• • • •

In Contra Country March 1988

"ARE YOU MISSIONARIES?" a European couple asks us at the Mexico City airport. We sure didn't look like we were going to Club Med. I am traveling with a peace group from Marin, California. Besides the mandatory Birkenstocks and sloppy dress, our group brings shovels, picks, saws, bags, boxes, mounds of stuff. I feel out of place. I am Banana Republic dressed. My travel companions are a bunch of sixties hippies gone to seed. We spend the first night in Mexico City. Our connecting flight to Nicaragua leaves tomorrow. Others went roaming but I stayed in, had dinner at the hotel.

My room is on the street level. Sounds of the city on a Friday night unfurl outside my window. Laughter, shouts, arguments, idle chatter. Patter of shoes matching voices, or silent voices, only the sound of the shoes clicking on the sidewalk. Cars pass, humming, screeching, honking. Tires whishing around corners. Scrunch and screeches. Doors slamming. Goodbyes said. Greet- ings made. Drifting in and out of sleep.

Morning in Mexico. I wake to the sound of hammering on metal. Pink! Pink! Pink! Bright sunlight strikes into my eyes. I squint at the sound across the street. At the entrance of a building under construction an old man squats. Cutting into the concrete walkway, head down, he intently watches the top of the chisel being struck by his heavy hammer. The worth of this man's labor stuns me. What it will take this man a day, a jackhammer could do in minutes.

By the time I get to Mexico City I've scoped out our group. They are boring. Why is it that peace people love meetings? Meetings several times before we leave, while we're waiting to leave, in Mexico City several times, and as soon as we land in Nicaragua. Screw them. I go sit in a corner. I travel to Nicaragua with this group because of price and where they are going. They had the cheapest rates and are going up near the Honduran border where I want to go.

Condega is where I spend seventeen of my twenty-five days in Nicaragua. Condega is on the left (west) side of Nicaragua, below the Honduran border some twenty miles.

It's cowboy country. I never saw so many cowboys. This dry part of Nicaragua is about real live cowboys who ride tiny, skinny horses. The hats, boots, spurs, everything looks cowboy. Horses match the cattle. Both like showing their ribs. Skinny, white, the cattle look like those in India and Africa. Long faced, a hump to their shoulder, tired cattle stand with hanging heads. Only their ears move, twitching the flies away. They range on hot, dry, scraggly, almost barren land peppered with chunks of porous black basalt rock. What little green there is winds the valley floor hugging the meandering, nearly dry river bed.

If Condega ever gains the status of New York, then the pension (boarding house) Baldovino where I stay will someday be overlooking Central Park. At the center of Nicaraguan towns or cities is always a park or town square, Spanish the influence. Ad- jacent would be one block for a church or cathedral. Retail shops, banks or government buildings frame the other three blocks around the town square. My humble hotel overlooks the town square and takes up half the block. In the evenings I watch the people do the paseo through the park. Next to the front steps of the Baldovino in a chair, I lean against the outside wall. Paseo, strolling men and women walk around sizing each other up.

But the Baldovino is not yet on Park Ave. Pigs and dogs roam free on the streets of Condega. They clean the place. Dust, dirt, swirls, twirls down earthen roadways. Streets are garbage cans. Drop it when ready. From banana peel to paper or whatever, people dump it on the street. Once a week citizens rake what remains in front of their homes into a pile and burn it. Fortunately, it's a biodegradable town.

Everyone is friendly. The dogs aren't, but they don't bother you either. Locals are of all colors, from blonde to black. Beautiful complexions, statuesque, when young Nica's are exceedingly handsome. Be it diet, be it lifestyle, the people age fast here. Maybe that's why there's so many kids. Kids are everywhere. It's as though the world here swallows adults. Lively, playful chil- dren, boys running everywhere chasing balls or rings, girls in twos or threes less obtrusive; both ever present.

Condega is also a town of guns, Ak-47's, rifles with big, long banana shaped clips coming out of the bottom curling forward. The citizens here are all armed. Everyone who wants one gets one. Each block in town stands an armed person on watch all night long, every night. This is Contra country.

Four thousand went to eight, the population of Condega doubled with the war. Farming and cattle are the industries of Condega. The third largest meat processing plant in Nicaragua sits a couple miles south of town. Besides a tannery and boot factory there is also a furniture plant. The meat processing plant and tannery are large operations, each employing several hundred. The other factories employ less than twenty.

Houses are of brick, wood, or adobe. Most have dirt flooring, some are tiled. Streets are all of dirt, some have a little gravel mixed in. Ruts, bumps, and gullies are especially prevalent on hilly sections of town. The only pavement is at the coffee drying plant just south of town. Each the size of a football field, bare rectangular cement pads meant for drying coffee beans sit white, vacant now, between seasons. Faint, an odor of coffee beckons from the warehouse.

You can walk around the whole town in a half hour. The Pan American highway borders one side, some rinky-dink river the other. The highway's rinky-dink too, just two narrow lanes of blacktop winding down the back of Nicaragua. El Arinal (S. the sandy place) is a tobacco growing cooperative four miles south of Condega. The Contra's attacked it a month earlier and killed the head of the cooperative. The Contras also shot and killed a small child. I guess killing the child was meant to emphasize their point; whatever that was.

The people from Marin have formed a sister city arrangement with Condega, unofficial of course. The group is supposed to build a memorial to the war dead in downtown Condega, across from the town square. Condega asked for help in building homes at El Arinal instead.

Condega has had over four hundred killed since the revolution. Four hundred out of a town of eight thousand, that's comparable to us losing over ten million during the Vietnam war.

This was the first town liberated by the Sandinistas in 1978.

It's just as well that I don't interface with the group. My concentration could be where I want it to be, with the people of Nicaragua. My major problem is language. My Spanish consists of a couple of semesters in college twenty-five years ago. I'm not sure I even passed the course. That's where Waldo comes in. I sit in a rocking chair on the veranda of the inner courtyard of the Baldovino, reading. It is evening. A man strolls by and stops.

"Oh. I see you're reading Steinbeck. What book is it?" he asks

"Travels With Charlie. Are you a Nicaraguense?" I respond. I am enjoying the luxury of light at night. So often the water and electricity are off here. It's the war.

"Oh yes, yes," Waldo's baritone plays to me, "I'm an Easterner." With that his chin juts out a bit more. "I have traveled as a seaman and worked for American and Canadian firms."

"And what do you do now?" I ask.

"I am the chief accountant at the meat plant. I've worked there the last fifteen years." Waldo is a black man. As with many from the east coast of Nicaragua, he speaks English. Slightly Caribbean his tone, tall, dignified, almost regal he carries himself. His hairline recedes up behind his ears, he's fifty-nine. Eyes of blue with the deepest gray give an intensity to his look. Blue eyes on a black man; far out. Well one eye anyway, the left eye is clouded over. It's cataracts.

Waldo always speaks in a precise, measured manner. The good eye and bad center a face framed in a perpetual pout. Waldo might laugh but never smiles. He always looks like he is ready to do Shakespeare. Either that, or a rendition of "Old Man River" in song.

Bitch, bitch, bitch, that's all Waldo ever does. His polite manner and style make ordinary whining seem mundane. I'm not sure if Waldo suffers to live or lives to suffer. Waldo does running criticisms of the government, the economy and mankind. His complaining is artistic, the style, the performance, the majesty of suffering. Waldo is a performer extraordinaire.

"Now tell me Ernie," his lead ins are an invitation to bear witness to the harshest tales of woe, his life one of such enormous hardships. He shows little interest in other matters, just his life, or lack thereof. He does this without really talking about himself. Circumstances, it is always the circumstances he finds himself in that cause his problems. Never is it his fault. I think the only time I see him betray his manner is when he talks of smoking.

"Look at these cigarettes we get here; it's trash." Contempt flashes in the good eye, silence stares from the bad one. He takes a quick deep drag on the Alas, Nica cigarette. "We get the stems and trimmings of the leaf. The good leaf is exported!" Hissing words exhale, mixed with the burned remnants of the product he detests. Smoking is a luxury in Nicaragua. Both men and women, even some children, when given the opportunity, love to smoke. American cigarettes are sipped like fine wine when smoked by a Nicaraguense.

Most of my time is spent with Waldo and the locals. For the most part I avoid the group. I can hear their type of complaining anytime. I need some new grief for a change. We spend most evenings in conversation, in rocking chairs, on the veranda of the inner courtyard of the hotel Baldovino. Not just Waldo and I, but his roommate, Panchito too. His real name is Raphael, but everyone calls him Panchito.

His home is in Leon, a city 200 miles away. Panchito lives at the Baldovino and goes home on weekends. He shares a small room with Waldo. Very Spanish are the roots of Panchito. Though you could see some Indian in him, Panchito shows mostly Spanish. His features are swarthy, curly hair frames a face with an aquiline nose. Mischievous, devilish eyes Panchito shows. His smile reveals his true side. He's a jokester.

Panchito is an educated man, the plant chemist at the matadora, slaughterhouse, where Waldo works. Panchito is 36, loves laughter and rum. He has a girlfriend in Leon, seen only on weekends. Rum is his daily passion. "Without rum there is no Panchito," he grins and nods to the wisdom of his own words. I never saw them noticeably drunk, but they drink every night.

In a dramatic gesture Waldo seems to rise up from his rocker. His hands slap down on the wide armrests. From deep within his throat, "Ah..uhh." Then his voice rises, "and shall we have a small shot Panchito?"

"Yes, Si my brother," a wide toothy grin breaks across Panchito's face. Rising together, Waldo speaks again.

"After you Panchito," Waldo bows gracefully at the waist and motions towards their doorway with a sweep of his left arm.

"Oh no my brother, after you." Panchito returns the bow and gestures palm up, the fingers of his right hand laid out as a tray.

"Would you be so kind Ernie? Please excuse Panchito and myself while we retire to have a small shot of rot gut rum." Waldo's good eye and deep voice hold my gaze. My nod gives recognition to a ritual played throughout the evening. Into their room, lit by a bare bulb suspended from the high-beam ceiling, they step. Just beyond the rough wooden doorway they stop. Into shot glasses the rum is poured. Then, facing each other glasses click, heads tilt back and arms flash hand to mouth. Panchito smacks his lips and dances a little salsa. Waldo stands, silent. The glasses are returned to the shelf, and out they saunter, Waldo always so regal, arms swaying precisely, Panchito a playful puppy just up from a nap.

Into the evening we talk. Waldo translating for Panchito. Panchito is trying to learn English. Our discussion is a series of jumbled words, gestures, and nods. They are both bewildered by my desire to visit a place like Condega.

"Please tell me Ernie," Waldo asks, "why would someone like you ever wish to come to a place like Condega? I cannot imagine what would possess you to come here to this." It is so easy isn't it; to look with eye so critical at others, then dissect, discern, and disgorge their truths so flippantly and quickly?

Sunshine came to visit me the other night. That's her name, honest. She's in her mid-forties, a big, raw-boned woman, hippy, hippy type, hairy armpits, legs, and all. She's one of the members of the group I travel with. Sunshine likes real loose sundresses, no bras, and books. She's nearly blind, always squinting through her thick glasses. If she isn't moving, she's reading all the time. Sunshine doesn't pay taxes. She tried to stop a Trident sub with a tiny rubber raft. It was up in Puget Sound some years back. Dressed in a wet suit, in a tiny raft, Sunshine took on the U.S. Navy, Coast Guard and whatever other Feds were available that day. A wave from the bow of the sub knocked her raft over. Coast Guard in boats, helicopters overhead, she's alone in the water, laid out on her back. Loudspeakers threaten to shoot her.

"I saw this beautiful light" she says.

My views on peace and life are what Sunshine says she wants when she comes to my room. I know she just wants to have sex with me. I play dumb. I don't say anything she doesn't know. She says she likes my phraseology and manner of delivery. I am the light so she can see her own self, she says. Maybe that's what we need in communication of this sort. Like baboons grooming, it's a process of verbal stroking. We need to reaffirm our common humanity. My reasons for coming to Nicaragua? It's time. I'm trying. To see. For myself. I don't believe until I see. I've got the burns to prove it. How can I be passionate about a place I've never seen? I don't want to have to answer the question, "have you been there?" with a 'no, but' response.

Nicaragua seems like a lie to me right from the start. I look at the pictures in the paper, on TV, poor peasants again. I know, but I still have to see it live once again. Sunshine leaves with just a hug and deep sigh.

My room at the Baldovino is the only one with a window and desk. We are talking primitive here. An old black wire to a bare light bulb hangs head high at the center of the room. Spartan furnishings, Washington slept in my bed. I haven't the foggiest what was used to stuff the mattress. Whatever it is or was it sure has hardened. Walls are of wide, rough, well-aged splin- tering planks. A whitewash done long ago has faded into the wood. Holes of various sizes, gaps, and cracks, preclude privacy. Doors have no latches, or locks.

I usually take breakfast at the Baldovino, always an egg, beans, rice, and a tortilla. Nicaraguan coffee is strong and gritty, like espresso. I try to do things in the mornings when the weather is tolerable. Long walks through town, along the river and into the hills I take, usually alone. Looking, listening, not speaking at all; I find such solace in my own quietness. It is so much easier to hear and see.

I meet an old man this morning, down at the edge of town. Fields of young beans and tomatoes border me along the dirt path I walk. Near the bank of the drying river our paths intersect.

He greets me warmly. His boots are of black rubber, white trousers and shirt, his dress. A sack is slung over his shoulder. The bad eye stands out, clouded over, cataracts again. We exchange greetings, the extent of my Spanish.

"No habla Español, senor," I say. He keeps right on talking, a bright smile on his face. A farmer of the earth, he's happy, on his way to work.

Most people are lean with a forlorn look, yet so dignified. The market has ten stalls in all. Vegetables green, red, white, brown, and yellow dominate the tables, pungent the aroma of onions. Fruit of the tropical variety, mangoes, papaya, and pineapple intermingle their aromas and presence. Meat draws a long line, but only shows once a week. Women do the selling, a few men hang about. The market is fenced and topped with barbed wire.

Martin, pronounced Marteen, is Donna Betty's grandson. Donna Betty owns the Baldovino. Basketball is Martin's passion. Tall for a Nica, maybe six feet or slightly more, he plays for team Condega. He and his sister Alioshia who is fifteen, live with Donna Betty. Martin's dad died an alcoholic, an endemic problem with Nicaraguan men. His mom, Donna Betty's daughter, lives in Honduras. Why? I do not know.

A senior in high school and seventeen, Martin will enter the military upon graduation. For two years he must serve. To be a Doctor of Medicine is his ambition. With Martin and his close buddies Jaime (James) and Jorge (George), Ann and I sit singing songs to one another. The heat has lifted. It's just after 9 pm. They sing in Spanish, we in English. Between songs we talk of dreams and the future. Ann translates well. She's a young woman from Vermont who has been building housing in Nicaragua for three months. Over in the central part of Nicaragua she has worked. Now she works on the El Arinal rebuilding project.

"And after your military service is over Martin, what do you think you will do?" I ask.

"Study medicine, be a doctor, and play basketball," he answers through Ann. Jaime wants to be an agricultural specialist. Jorge has not decided.

Jaime plays the guitar as does Ann. The church bells start just after Martin and Jaime begin singing.

"Attack!" Jaime yells jumping up. The young boys run home. Donna Betty slides shut the bolt of the large wooden doors. Sounds of the metal bolt sliding through the locking hinges ring in the lobby of the pension.

"She asks that you go get everyone and have them come into her living room. She says it is safest there." Ann says looking over at me, while translating Donna Betty's request. In the lobby we stand together, a kerosene lamp illuminating our silence. I don't have to do much rounding up. The people are all out of their rooms. I don't have a feeling of danger. After getting my flashlight from my room I join the others.

The town has gone black. Military jeeps roar by, their lights jerking to the bounce of the rutted streets. Upon the tiled floor, against the hard wall of Donna Betty's living room, I sit pensively. Glass louvered windows overlook the town square. Ann and Lloyd kneel, peering out of them. Donna Betty is sobbing quietly, hunched in a chair. Before I realize his presence, he is upon me. From the shadows of the darkened house he emerges, the rifle held at his side, the ammo pouches on his chest. Jesus Christ! It's Martin. We wait for several hours. Nothing happens.

Before returning to my room, I go up on the roof where Martin stands guard. With his elbows on the chest high wall bordering the rooftop patio Martin leans, gazing out into the night. Clouds guard the stars. The dark rifle stands next to him. He looks at me as I step up beside him. I cannot see his eyes, only his nod. For but a moment I stay, then say, "buenas noche, Martin."

"Buenas," Martin answers. A boy only hours earlier, now a man to me. Guns do make the man, don't they?

Martin is tired this morning. He was up all night guarding us. He's on his way to school, wonder if he'll play basketball today? Martin goes to a Catholic school. The Institute it's called. Blue and white uniforms are worn, that's how you always spot Catholics, uniforms.

The attack was a false alarm. It's our American 82nd Airborne running around the Honduran border that caused it. Too bad we don't realize what we do to guys like Martin.

Unquestionably, the major influence in town is the Catholic church, yet not one of the priests in town is Nicaraguan. There's a Mexican, an Argentine and some other South American; but no Nicaraguan.

John and I go for a walk down to the farms that line the river on the south side of town. Little boys 5-7 years old start to assemble around us. Like little dogs that slowly ease on up to you, sniffing, slinking, testing. John asks to take a picture of them with me. That did it, they come alive.

We walk onward towards the river. It's the height of the dry season now, not much water. Hyacinths choke the few sections where water pools. Several cows munch lazily. We ask the boys where to cross. Excitedly they wave us on. If you want to excite a small boy, make him feel important. On the other side of the river a small dirt path leads to a small ranch. Skins hang out to dry, a small cattle pen.

Then they start. They know our Spanish is almost nonexistent. They are excitedly chattering to us since we gave them control of the situation by asking them how to cross the river. The largest or oldest does most of the talking. With curly hair and flailing arms, he chatters constantly. He sounds like a car trying to start. Number two boy fills in the gaps with his own perceptions or clarifications. His style is more reflective. He does not gesture. His eyes do not blink like number one. He thinks he is interpreting for the bigger boy.

Aqui? Aqui? They keep pointing to various trail routes. We begin climbing into the hills. *Mira, mira,* they point out various things, citing its name in Spanish. Repeating the name until I repeat it. Then when satisfied, *sí* and on to another.

One brings me a small dry piece of shit. *Cameron* he keeps saying. I pull out my Spanish dictionary. Rabbit.

"Paloma" he cries out when a dove flushes from the brush.

Over and across fields we troop. A field trip, a tour with guides scattering around and in front of us. A large outcropping dominates.

"They say you can see well from up there," John says.

"Bueno" I say and motion. Like Marines scattering in a fire fight they spread, attacking the hill, each trying to reach the top first. Around the scratchy brush they are practically running. At the top, a panoramic

view of Condega. It sits in a depression. Hills and ridges lining the outsides. No wonder it's extra hot here. It might have a smog problem someday if progress comes. But not now. How quaint it all is. Mans' intrusion not so intrusive.

It is then that reality returns for me. The boys begin talking of the Contra attacks and the threatened bombing the night before. A Contra CIA plane flew over the night before. Anti-plane missiles going off. Everyone in the town scattering, shooting. With eyes so alive number one gestures and speaks wildly.

All the other boys join in except little snot nose. He attaches himself to me early on. I'm used to that. Certain guys take a shining to me and I recognize it in him right off. With such men it is not necessary for me to say anything. It is a feeling we share, a simpatico. As the other boys vent their fears, I feel his finger hook into my left pocket. He wants to hang on to me. I look down at him. He's staring up at me, eyes wide open, lips shaking. A line of snot forms in layers of crust from his nostrils to his upper lip. Slowly and softly in almost a whisper he begins to vent his fears to me. I cup his head with my left hand. He leans into me. We stand together silent for a while. I am with the enemy. This is who is terrifying us? I wonder if our children could handle repeated terror so well. Perhaps it just takes practice. Thoughts of war are left there.

Excitedly they return to their guided tour as we leave the hillock and descend back into town.

I ride one day with the young Mexican priest. He drives a four-wheel drive truck that is almost new. We go into the hills to gather palm fronds for the upcoming Easter service of Palm Sunday. We traverse roads barely passable to horse, or donkey. To shacks of dark dry wood, he points. On baren hills hang small, rickety homes of the poor. It is from this pool of humanity that the Contra's get their recruits.

"They come at night and kidnap the young men," the priest says without emotion. "With guns, they shoot up the place and take the young men, sometimes a young woman too." He speaks these things as though it were a well-known fact of life. It is news to me.

• • • •

Loneliness

WALNUT CREEK 1988

All alone do I possess thee? It is a mystery to me from where you come. Certainly, I did not request your company. Companions yes but not friends are we. When with you the world seems less clear. The sky is never bright even when blue and cloudless. Things move by and around me unnoticed. In almost a trance my business of living is conducted. Sullen, you wait at my every departure from your attention.

Silence seems to pervade my being even when I know the sounds abound about me. It is a stillness you bring with you that only allows clear attention to be directed to you. You cloak me as we walk together, like a coarse scratchy coat against my bare flesh. You dominate with your presence. May I ask that you leave?

So familiar I am with you, I fear the loneliness of your departure. You mask and swirl away my past memories. It is as though I have only known my life with you; so total is your possession. And what my dear companion will it be to drive you away once again? A gentle breeze that strokes my cheek and whispers into my ear, or a quiet dawn that fills the sky with light that my eye cannot deny? Or perhaps it will be a hello, a face, a smile that reminds me of love once known. Whenever you're ready. Don't bother to shut the door behind you. I know you'll return at your calling.

• • • •

Plans

WALNUT CREEK 1988

One thing you cannot accuse me of, is lack of planning. I plan the living shit out of my life. So many sleepless nights spent plotting the minutest possible scenarios to events that never take place. Even more incredible, my energy gets wasted on junk that increases my neuroses. Agonizing over what other people might think and care about me, as if one could ever hope to be so important to others. I am that fucking stupid.

It's a perfect set-up. I can never win. Like the mouse on the treadmill, the dog chasing its tail; it looks real as hell until I step outside myself and take a look at what I am doing for and to myself.

Now I do what I can to protect my remaining sanity. I try to laugh as much as possible.

I think if there is a heaven then I'll get to sit around and watch the VCR tapes on the most personal moments of others. I sure as hell know how fucking stupid and silly I've been playing out my fantasies. Hey, the real trip would be if we not only get to watch but also get to listen to what goes on in the minds of others. I know that's where I really do my tripping. I'd be dead if all the stuff I dream about really happens. Wooooo!

I am so concerned about what others feel about me. If I can figure others out then I'd know myself. Problem is that all the other clowns are playing the same game. Most people are just like me. They don't give a shit about me just like I don't give a shit about them. Why don't they love me? I want first crack at the tit of life. Why should I share? They wouldn't share with me.

Ah sweet fear. How dear my fear. What would life be with- out you? One thing for sure, I wouldn't need to plan.

. . . .

My Last War 1991

This article was printed in Vietnam Generation Journal and
Newsletter, V3 N3, November 1991

I'VE DONE THREE WARS and I've had enough. I survived
Vietnam. I was a founder of Nuremberg Actions out at the Concord
Naval Weapons Station where I helped win one against the Gipper,
during his pathetic incursion into Nicaragua. Yea team! But I got my
ass kicked bad in this last one. So I'm hanging up the guns America.
Fuck it. You turds are on your own.

"I don't give a shit what you say Ernie, you was on patrol out there
at Orinda," Jerry my shrink said to me. I had just agreed to let myself be
institutionalized for the next seven or eight months in a VA hospital.
I'm glad ole Georgie and that halfwit partner of his, Danny boy, think
that the Vietnam Syndrome is behind us. As usual though, we fucked
up Vietnam vets have failed to get the word. There is a long waiting list
to get into the PTSD program.

"Don't feel bad, Ernie," Jerry my shrink said to me, "the Gulf War
fiasco done stirred up a whole lot of shit for all of us." Jerry is a blood,
disabled Vietnam vet and VA Vet Center counselor. He had just
recounted for me how he went berserk while in a barber shop. It was
the afternoon that CNN broke the story live, on TV. Some Korean war
vet started cheering. I don't have to give you the details, but after Jerry
got done telling the clown what he does for a living and what he has to
see every day, the guy apologized. Profusely.

What was I doing at the Orinda Bart station that Jerry claims was a
"patrol?" Just vigiling. I swear to god, I was just standing silently with a
few other peaceniks, holding a sign, when I got assaulted. Two weeks in
a row. Back in '87 we called ourselves the CONCORD FOUR. Every
evening Lloyd, Margie, Jean, and myself would meet out at the tracks
and silently vigil. I resisted getting involved actively in this latest noble
cause of ours as long as I could. Shit, man, if there's one thing that

Vietnam taught me it's the survival one. All the flags waving, yellow ribbons and women having their first orgasms in god knows how long, while singing God Bless America, told me I had better stay low and shut up. But I'm an old sentimentalist and a soft touch. When the shelter in Baghdad got bombed and I watched America's denial (blame the victim), I felt obligated. Yes, I know. I'm codependent. Lloyd was enraged. He called and suggested we reform the Concord Four. I felt like Gary Cooper going out there to Orinda Bart, the first time, on February 13. Yes, I know, an unlucky number. Why Orinda? Because Lloyd and Jean live there and it's the wealthiest neighborhood on the BART system. "The belly of the beast," as my girlfriend Pat said. I had dusted off my old piece, my weapon, and held it up for the public to see. "Veterans for Peace," is what it says. I am a provocative fucker aren't I? We showed up for the evening rush hour. Five to six-thirty p.m. Boy did we piss people off. But, as usual, we said nothing. It was too much for one upstanding businessman in a suit and tie. Donald Stone, besides the obscenities and the finger in my face, tried to punch me out. Too bad for Donnie this old gunslinger is an ex-pug. His round house punches caught arms only. Yeah, I still remember how to keep em up high. What I didn't do was counter. Oh, he was so open for my famous overhand right, but I didn't. I don't know what's happened to me, but I've become an absolute sissy in my old age. I calmly called him brother and let him go. And of course the police show up after it's all over. I was so cavalier when I declined to press charges.

I had a very troubling series of dreams the night before week two. In it my lieutenants kept coming to me in the battle dress crying and hugging me. They kept telling me how much they loved and needed me. As usual, I was in a bar, the officers club, I think. I kept reassuring them that their old skipper would take care of them. I was in civvies. I was macho. I was 'the Man' once again. Two of my lieutenants from Vietnam had written from the Gulf, around Christmas time. Their letters were very nostalgic. They're colonels now and were getting ready to lead their regiments into battle. They knew it was coming. And yes, they know their ole skipper is a fucking peace nut. It don't matter to them, they know what I did for them when it counted. You'd be surprised how understanding marines can be sometimes.

I had a bad feeling about going out to Orinda on February 20, week two of our once-a-week vigil. But Margie called and she was counting on me being there. Margie's a former Marine. She's not too macho. A real sweet grandmother, in fact. But she is addicted to peace. So I'm an enabler, I guess. I carry my feelings on my face. When I showed up at BART with my girlfriend Pat, Lloyd and the rest of our gang was already there. Lloyd took one look at me and said, "What's wrong, brother?"

"I don't know Lloyd, I got a bad feeling about this," I said. It had been so long, I had forgotten. Towards the end of my tour in Vietnam (twenty-three years ago), I had honed my senses to the point that I had become psychic. I knew when we were going to get hit and I was always prepared. I now attributed my feelings to the dreams I'd had the night before. Wrong. I watched Donald come down the escalator. We stood about 75 feet beyond the exit stations. He didn't see us until he went through the exit. Bingo! He went ballistic. Oh, dear friends, if looks could kill. He was carrying a big, heavy briefcase and reached in and threw something that was plastic. Then he changed the briefcase to his right hand and started in with the middle finger of left like he was trying to masturbate his nose. He walked behind Helen who was on the left end of our short gray line and nailed her from the back, with his briefcase. Lloyd and I, being the two males, played our roles. We broke ranks and moved toward Helen. "Stop," Lloyd shouted. Donnie nailed Lloyd with his briefcase. Then, as though in a trance, he came onto me. I can only imagine what a woman being raped must feel like. He broke my finger on the first swing of his briefcase. Stupid me, my hands were open, instead of shut like I'd been taught. After several more blows from Donald I made an on-the-spot decision.

"Sir," I said, "This is two weeks in a row that you've as- saulted me. I'm placing you under citizen's arrest." He went calm when I embraced him. I took him up against the wall and that is when it happened. What's it?

What really fucked me up in Nam was not the gunfights, which I had mentally prepared myself for. What fucked me up was what I had not prepared myself for, the shelling I had to take for 77 days at Khe Sanh, without being able to fight back. A BART employee in blue uniform started screaming, "Let him go! Let him go! You've got no right to arrest anyone." This incited the crowd, that turned into a mob, and it gave silent Donald new courage. The mob went absolutely bullshit. Businessmen in suits and stylishly dressed business women circled me while I straddled Donald. Their screams filled the gentle Orinda air.

"You're a fucking traitor," they so proudly screamed, "We're telling the police that you started all this." I was so distracted that I didn't even do beaver shots on the women that loomed over me, circling, looking for an opening to kick me. And that is when 'it' happened. I've never done wide awake flashbacks until then. NVA in full battle dress became superimposed over the figures of America's upstanding citizens in proper business attire. Then my old daemon from Vietnam screamed at me.

My daemon in Vietnam was my "second voice." It would guide me as I'd lead my rifle company on patrol. It would question me, by pointing out danger areas, things to be concerned with. "Who is the enemy!" that old voice kept screaming to me as the figures of my old enemy kept flashing on and off the businessmen and women, who circled me like a pack of angry wolves. "Who is the enemy?" Indeed. No one got in a kick. There's one other thing about me that I'm noted for. "The look." I've had guys that tried to take me on during my old brawling days say after the fight that they knew I was going to kick their ass. My look hypnotized them. I kept making eye contact with those brave American warriors in suits and ties and they'd back up every time I did so. As soon as the police drove up, all those brave Americans disappeared like Danny did during Vietnam.

The cops took our statements, cited Donald, and let him go. "Don't worry," the BART cop reassured me. "He's got real good IDs, and I told him if he did it again we'll arrest him." How reassuring that was. He also told me that he'd turn it over to the DA and they would contact me to hear my side. Having been the victim of the Contra Costa County's District Attorney's office during my Concord days, I'm sure you all realize how confident I was that justice would prevail. Peace makes one so cynical, doesn't it?

As the trauma of the event began to wear off, the pain took over. Yes my friends, there is an adrenaline rush in combat and when I flashed back I got a good dose. I didn't even realize my finger was broken, my back and neck severely strained and I was full blown PTSD until several hours later. But, when I came down, what a crash.

After Jerry listens to the story, he tells me that it was me that was responsible for my condition. "How many different ways do you know how to kill people, Ernie?" he asks.

"How many ways are there?" I respond.

"Exactly," he says. "Ernie, you're a dangerous weapon just waiting to go off and one of these days one of them assholes out there is going to push you too far and you're going to really lose control. It's time for you to go into the hospital, my man." That prick made me break down and cry when I realized that I have no power over this monster that possesses me.

"But, Jerry," I pleaded, "I been working on my shit for six fucking years now."

"Yeah, well it ain't been enough," he said. "And you got to learn to stay away from that shit that can trigger our condition. What would have happened to those fucking cowards in business suits if you'd have been carrying your M-16 Automatic, there would have been a whole lot of dead motherfuckers out there in Orinda, right?" Who am I to argue with my shrink? So I'm going to get my PhD in PTSD. I'm waiting to get into Menlo Park which for Nam guys is the equivalent of a law degree from Harvard or Boalt Hall. And fuck you George.

P.S. I checked and found out that the DA's office was going to let Donald off with just a terrible tongue lashing. Yancy was probably going to lick his ass. So I did my duty and went down to let them know that I was not just some hippie scum, like they think we all are. I took with me copies of the letters from my lieutenants. They let me talk to the newest assistant DA. He had just started a month ago. When he read the loving letter from one of my lieutenants on the official Marine stationery, he almost fell out of his chair. "Holy shit," he said. "I was an artillery FO with 1/4." 1/4 is one of the battalions commanded now by my former lieutenant. There's more. This new DA is a Latino. I'm Asian. He thanked me for "paving the way for guys like me to become officers in the Corps." I was the first if not only Korean rifle company commander in Nam. I told him about how his DA's office had all the time in the world to arrest me and book me and jail me during the Concord times. But now when I come to the DA to request that Mr. Stone be charged with violating my civil rights, his office won't do a thing. "Can you believe what that mob did to me at Orinda," I asked him?

"Yeah, man," he angrily said, "I can't believe it. Them rich white folks with silver spoons in their mouths ain't got any of their kids or grandkids over there fighting. It's guys like you and me that's got to do it for them."

"Brother," I said, "if you feel that way, how can you handle it?"

"I just close my eyes to it," he said. "I concentrate on what I got to do to make it." He seemed so sad. I didn't let up now that I had his attention.

• • • •

Kicking the Vietnam Syndrome 1991

THIS WAS EXCERPTED from articles published in Vietnam Veterans of America, Inc. California State Council in Service to America Volume 4 Issue 3 and 4, under the pseudonym Thomas Meade.

The Gulf War got me like it did a lot of other Nam guys. I went full blow again.

"You're not crazy," Dr. P., the Psychiatric Inpatient Unit (PIU) psychologist, screamed at me. "PTSD (post-traumatic stress disorder) is not insanity."

"Then why in the hell have you got us here with these lunatics?" I screamed back at him. PTSD is all about rage and anger. I was doing a venting. Like a long-submerged leviathan, I spewed my anger at Dr. P. I hated admitting that my life had finally come to this. I'm in a psychiatric ward for Christ's sake. Talk about hitting your bottom. Dr. P. kept trying to reassure me.

"PTSD is just a normal reaction to an abnormal situation," he said softly. "What happened to you guys in Vietnam was a fucking outrage. It was a goddamn fucking tragedy. Everything about it was fucked. Its reason, our country's reaction, you guys did the best you could and our country let you down." This guy swears more than me.

"Fuck America!" I screamed.

PIU, Psychiatric Inpatient Unit, is feared and hated by the rest of the hospital. And the guys with PTSD are feared and hated by the general psych patients.

Ft. Miley is a teaching hospital. Psychiatrists do three months of a four-year residency. Ft. Miley was once a real fort. Old circular bunkers of smooth concrete built one hundred years ago, now lie abandoned. Gun positions that had guarded the southern entrance to San Francisco Bay still cover the sea side of the old fort, but the guns and crews are long gone. I feel a vague, low intensity stirring in my gut. I remember a place long ago called Khe Sanh, with such a fog and many large guns. It made perfect sense with the old gun positions and the student shrinks. So Freudian.

They knew I was a writer when they admitted me. I was sent to Ft. Miley for having homicidal and suicidal tendencies and thoughts. I didn't want VA drugs. I was afraid they would ruin my creativity. I was wired and pissed off when they admitted me.

I got discharged after a month at Miley. They told me my bed was needed. I just wasn't crazy enough for Miley's standards. I didn't know if I should feel proud or ashamed. They told me Menlo could take me in two months. They told me to stay cool and on their drugs while I waited. I could get all the refills I needed. Whoopee.

Menlo Park is not a park. Menlo Park is a town south of San Francisco known as Silicon Valley. According to the VA I was in The National Center For the Treatment of Post-Traumatic Stress Disorder. There are seven hundred beds at VA Medical Center Menlo. PTSD patients are given ninety. Beds is how our loving VA refers to we veterans. We're not a person, just a slot in a ward, a bed.

Guzman is the head honcho. Guzman has sold the VA a line of very expensive bullshit. He claims he and his wonder team can rehabilitate a street vet with this wondrous new therapy called Process and Focus. The Guzman theory of vet handling entails surrender.

"If you do not surrender to the program, the program will not work," he says. Right. Neither would have Jim Jones program in Guyana worked, without surrender.

Guzman strikes me as the quintessential Vietnam wanna-be. He did an Air Force ground tour, back in the world, during Vietnam. He somehow managed to duck the real tour. The guy has no personal experience with combat. This does not however prevent him from claiming to be the guru of PTSD.

I knew the program was bullshit the first week I was there. Control is what motivates the collective egos of Guzman and his senior staff of all white, guilt driven, sadistic, emotionally disturbed, anal retentive males. Twenty-three days was more than enough time for me to see that the ones with the severest emotional problems were some of the staff members. Guzman is the sickest of them all. He is hated by patients and staff. I never heard a positive thing said about him.

When you check into the PTSD program the first thing you lose is your dignity. You're required to wear VA issued pajamas. Every moment of your day is dictated. If you play their game you can get into your own clothes in four to five weeks. You have to earn the right to get out of your pj's.

I watched my first treatment review, when they tried to break Chief. He is a proud Apache. At his interrogation by the staff and his fellow vets, Chief refused to play the white man's game.

"You guys are hiding under Donna's skirt," Chief said and pointed at nurse Ratched (Donna). Donna was leading the assault on Chief. His "brother" vets had joined in on his evaluation. Chief grinned and fired verbal darts back at his supposed brother Vietnam vets. Chief was not taking the feedback. Taking the feedback is where people can say anything they want about you and you're not allowed to respond. Treatment review is a cruel game played out at the direction of a sadistic staff.

"I must be from a different planet," was how I opened my critique of Chief. The staff was not impressed when I spoke up for Chief and his kind. "I must be from a different planet," I repeated, "because I don't see Chief at all like the rest of you do." Then I had the audacity to call Chief "brother." I could see people wince when I said that. I'd committed a mortal sin in coming to Chief's defense. Tsk. Tsk. Word went out that I was forming a racial breakaway group. Yeah, like me and a few Indians were going to pull a Custer at Menlo.

I admitted that I felt a special bond with native peoples. I accused the program of treating Indians in a disrespectful manner.

"This is an Anglo program," I said while evaluating Chief. "If anything we should be asking his people how to heal." I was assigned to toilet cleaning duty the next day.

Even Vietnam vets, notoriously the most independent of thinkers, are vulnerable to mind fucking. Brother feeding on brother during treatment review proved it for me. I guess I'm one of those old-fashioned types. I like to follow the golden rule. Treatment review is just another form of attack therapy. To me it's another form of violence. There is not a damn thing nice about it. It is demeaning.

Don't let anyone tell you differently. Drugs are the heart of the VA mental health system. Drugs frame everything else. The drug cart is the first thing you see in the morning and last thing you see at night. Mellow is what the VA wants in patient behavior. Forget the classes and sessions, they're bullshit. It's the drugs that get results the VA wants. The VA could care less about the patient needs. Patients are watched and reported on 24 hours a day.

"How are you doing, Mr. Spencer?" Paul the day nurse asked me one day.

Always noted for my honesty, I replied, "I can't sleep here. I hate this place." That night my dose of Nortriptyline, a mood enhancer, was doubled. No consultation, no discussion, they just dropped an extra pill in my shot cup of evening meds. I flashed back to Grace Slick doing White Rabbit, raised an eyebrow and asked, "What's this?"

"Of course you can refuse your additional medication, Mr. Spencer," MaryAnn, the gray-haired wicked witch night nurse snapped at me. How dare I, a lowly nut, question the VA. The problem with Nortriptyline is that it always left me feeling hung over. I'd feel woozy in the morning. MaryAnn was pissed not because she gave a damn about my taking the extra pill or not, she just didn't want to have to do the paperwork. The VA has some unbelievable lazy people on the payroll.

The biggest joke at Menlo is the therapy session called Process. Patients arriving around the same time are bunched into groups of ten to twelve. Those that graduate from Process move on together to the big time called Focus.

Sometimes while at Process I felt as though my muse was on the wall across from my seat laughing its ass off. Life is short. I felt like I was wasting my time having to sit and watch two pathetic VA employees bullshit us about feelings for an hour and a half. I was trying my best to give the program a chance, but the bullshit just overwhelmed me.

Not all the staff at Menlo are heartless. Mary Anne, the head nurse, is nice. She runs the weekly class called Autobiography. Each guy has to give his pre-military autobiography before he goes on to Focus. Focus is supposed to deal with one's war traumas. Mary Anne's style is gentleness.

Every guy that I heard give his autobiography had abuse done to him when he was a child. Violent families are fertile breeding grounds for the Armed Forces, it seems. I heard story after story of parental alcoholism or insanity, beatings, and religious fanaticism. I watched Mary Anne wince as middle-aged men recalled their appalling pasts as children. You could see the tears well up in her eyes as she blinked to try to stay clear.

I have nothing in common with those men's childhoods. I got my bell rung in Vietnam, period. Vietnam is where I got my PTSD. My mom and dad have always loved me and never hurt me. The guys I heard give their autobiographies were PTSDed before they got out of grade school. One guy referred to himself as part of a litter. His father treated him that way. Unbelievable shit they told. Violence is bred into children and passed on. If what I saw is any indication, violence is a very serious problem in America.

The schedule at the VA program is numbing. It's a dreary repetition of meals, classes, and meds that break you down. The last thing they want you to do in a VA mental hospital is think. That's what the staff fears most. Private thoughts are dangerous thoughts. I felt like I was a POW while I was there. I've been accused of a lot of things in my life, but stupid was never one of them. I've always had a nose for bullshit. The PTSD program at Menlo is bullshit. The only reason most guys stay is because of the money they can get. How much? About 10 to 12 grand tax free. The guys get paid about seventeen hundred bucks a month in disability pay from the VA. Privately run programs can and do outperform the inefficient VA system. Private health care facili- ties provide superior care for a fraction of the cost. The best argument I know of for national health insurance is the VA. Wouldn't that be something? If we had national health insurance we could disband the VA. It is estimated that at least 300,000 Vietnam vets suffer from PTSD. In ten years Menlo Park has handled barely six thousand.

What blew me out was the treatment review they did on Wild Phil. Phil was a POW for two years during the Korean War. He acts the clown to mask his pain.

"I thought I talked to you in confidence, Nancy," Phil asked in a perturbed manner. Nancy was not only his private counselor, she was also conducting his treatment review.

"There's no secrets here," Nancy said. Then she quickly assumed the offense. "How are you feeling now, Phil?" At this point Rick, the head of our ward became very excited. He began pacing back and forth in an agitated manner. A sick sneer spread across his face. Phil began shaking.

"What the hell are you people doing?" Phil asked. He looked bewildered. "OK, you want to know? OK—I propped up a dead man for two days, so's I could eat his chow," Phil yelled out. He ran to the farthest part of the room and perched like a bird on a chair. His sobs were gruff and snotty. He began an eerie wail.

I looked around the room and saw the collective look of shock on the faces of the patients.

"It's OK, Phil," Nancy said. That's when I lost it.

"It's not OK," I screamed at her.

"Hush, Ernie," she said, trying to control my rising temper. That's when I went off.

"It's not fucking OK," I sneered and said again to her.

Rick rushed to Phil. Phil shook and whined and waved a limp hand, like a broken wing. His eyes showed a terror that seemed to hypnotize Rick. As he knelt before Phil, Rick stared in awe. It seemed some sort of mystical event to him. I think he might have even had an orgasm. Rick could hardly contain himself. In less than two months, he and his wondrous team had broken a man who carried his pain privately for over forty years.

I packed my bags and demanded the keys to my truck. They had my truck in an impound lot and kept my keys under lock and key. They make it as hard as possible for you to leave.

"Can I walk with you to security?" a guy calls himself a doctor asked. Dondershine had more time as a used car salesman than in medicine. Along the way he convinced me to stop off at his office. He tricked me by lying.

"Look, tell the truth now. Do you want to go out in traffic in the condition you're in? What right do you have to endanger innocent people?" He then promised to help. "Look, how about taking a shot of Melloril. It's a wondrous drug that will calm you down. It won't make you sleepy. You can drive in half an hour, I promise," he said and smiled.

He gave me two shots of this white liquid and sixteen hours later I woke up in a locked ward. I was groggy and stumbled when I stood up.

I told the nurse on duty that if they didn't let me go I was going to break something. It was a Saturday. Only one doctor had to cover the entire Menlo facility. I waited several hours before Big Bertha came to see me.

"Do you half suweeside inclination," she asked in a very pronounced German accent. "Do you vish to do bodily halm to anzee one?"

I felt like saying nein, but answered instead with a simple, "no." Before they let me leave I had to sign a VA form that said I was leaving because I was completely crazy. The form was a VA classic. It said I must be irrational. It said that the VA had done everything in its power to help me. I also had to agree that I was fully responsible for whatever crazy shit I might do. I signed the form D. Quayle and left.

. . . .

Cuba 1995

I GO TO THE AIRPORT with Auntie Ruth and Pat. Meet Pam the organizer from Global Exchange, Jim and one or two others. We leave for Houston at 1 AM November 8. In Houston for three hours then to Cancun. Global has the grease and connections. They hold the Cubana flight for us—walk us around and through Mexican customs—put us on the airline first. It's a cluster fuck—Jesus—people bringing all kinds of shit on. No FAA rules apply—baggage and shit on the floors. Russian jet could barely take off. Hot, hot, hot until we are 30 minutes airborne.

Great treatment at Havana Jose Marti airport. We are celebrities. Cuban TV covers the Yanqui veterans coming to Cuba to protest the embargo. I hang back. At the airport we meet Esmeralda, our interpreter. She tells me people think she's part Chinese.

"You Chinese too?" she asks with a smile. I'm not sure if she's hitting on me or just naturally friendly. We are met by Arnaldo Tamayo, the Cuban astronaut.

Havana is clean and orderly, needs paint but I am impressed by its quietness. Our hotel is run by the education department. With the need for foreign cash each segment of the social order has to come up with ways to get money. We're in a nice section of Havana one block from the beach. The room is clean and humble, shower has a "hot" water adapter. Thing runs through a contraption like an overhead douche kit—water gets warm just as I finish my shower.

At dinner, the astronaut talks very clearly through our interpreter Esmeralda (Hope). Arnaldo is a Cuban hero. First black in space. He's quite impressive. He honestly talks about Cuba's one party system and how it's democratic. Each interest area— farmers, intellectuals—have their own subunits. He frankly talks about how the collapse of the Soviet Union hurt economically. Everyone then introduces themselves. Your usual run of the mill peace activists.

There's a couple here from Santa Rosa, California that I know from the Concord Naval Weapons days. Bill and Jean. He's WWII. They remember me and especially my book.

Dinner is chicken and rice, fruit cocktail before, and some sort of sweet thing with cheese after. I go to the bar with Jim and two other Nam guys. Crystal beer is $.85.

I get a call from Associated Press out of Mexico. Talk to Sarah, who wants to know something about why I'm doing this. I give her my usual smart-ass spiel. "What's the issue?" I ask.

"Communism? Look at China. We're trading with them." Blah, blah, blah. Jees, I hope my dad reads me in the Honolulu paper. I say I am originally from there. Back at the bar with a guy named Dave, ex-marine, who lost both legs in an ambush. He works with VVA Foundation, setting up prosthesis places around the world, Cuba, El Salvador, Cambodia, Angola.

The next day we tour Havana on old bikes with the group and university students. Havana has a great ambience; what a perfect way to see the place. It seems so orderly and not slow but calm. We stop at a grade school and I'm amazed by the vitality of the children. They learn by playing, dancing, singing, doing their consonants. I could hardly keep myself from crying. The beauty of the children treated as a treasure. All are fed. They do their own lessons as much as possible. One little girl with crossed eyes attracts me—she has such life, such vitality. She will be a beautiful woman someday. The teachers stand outside the circles as the kids lead their own lessons. They lead their own exercises. We brought a donation of school supplies and every class wants to perform songs and skits for us.

Old Havana is being rebuilt. They're using local labor with joint foreign contracts. They're trying to preserve the character. Foreign tourists are all over, Italian, Spanish, German, Canadians. This place is going to take off.

Afternoon. We meet with Cuban vets, all colonels, and gen- erals. How important can we be? It humbles me. It angers me. America has such power over the world, yet the world so wants to get along. Perhaps only in poverty is it possible to understand. We have so much yet we lack a basic understanding of social courtesy. Our arrogance is irrational. It's because of fear. The more things you have the more fucked up you become. I wish I knew how to share this but fear I would be pissing in the wind. We're too out of touch to understand.

We leave for Guantanamo tomorrow.

The flight down on a Russian jet is not too bad. Drink great rum, get wild. Seven-year-old rum! We see a banana plantation. Meet college professors, engineers, and all black work.

At the cultural center a woman, Mariana C, mother of Antonio and Jose M, blows off the guys telling her to speed up, as she describes the murals painted on the wall. A hospital, rustic, very clean with a lack of essential medicines has 865 beds and 2,000 plus staff. Mothers of children stay at the hospital to nurse their child.

"We put all emphasis on our children first, every single one," Mariana tells us. WWII John makes an ass of himself again at the meeting at the hospital. Fuckers with private agendas piss me off. Preaching to the choir again. Stress and heat get to our Cuban in- terpreters. They snap at and correct each other during translation.

Wild Afro-Haiti dance and drum show at the hotel that night. Women do very suggestive dances. I write my speech for Guantanamo Bay.

Today I see what we called Gitmo from a high peak on the windward side. It is bigger than I thought it would be. I feel a serenity come over me looking through the binoculars at where I was stationed for five months almost thirty years ago. The salt flats I hated. Patrols, ambushes, my young innocence of that time comes back. But I don't feel anger or frustration over who I was then—the young macho fool. I am at the point where "those issues" are now fully forgotten. I notice that I do not feel the need for more than a cursory look at the leeward side where I was. It is not that I am tired of it, but more a sense that my mind and heart have better things that "they" desire.

The flight back from Gitmo to Havana is a pisser again. 32 passenger Russian built jet like the one we took to Gitmo. Everyone drinking, laughing, arguing. James, the videographer, asks if I mind letting him shoot me. Near a window on the setting sun side, I blow him away. What now seems so matter of fact to me has such power over people. I must be very cautious about this gift or curse. I'm not sure whether I should start to speak out or continue to hold back. After he videos me, James, a psychotherapist, asks if I mind talking about some of my Vietnam experiences.

"Sure, no problem," I say. He's a PTSD therapist. I am fine but he is crying away. I tell him I'll send him my book and Khe Sanh reunion video. Bet it drops him good when he reads the book or watches the video.

At Gitmo the Cuban locals have a memorial service for their war dead. From their Angola war, all those who are KIA (killed in action) are interred at the same memorial site. Not a bad idea when you think about it. They have a "wall" with all the names, and the guys right there. Good way to draw attention at one point about the price of war.

That night after dinner, I go for a beer and end up at Maceo Diaz's house across the street. These folks have taken to the Vets for Peace in a big way. Maceo is a retired lieutenant colonel and gets by now raising chickens to sell the eggs and has a garden for vegetables. We end up telling war stories to one another. He has gun time fighting the Miami rebels who came back after Somoza went to Angola and Mozambique. I learn from him that one Cuban was killed in North Vietnam. Guy was a missile observer and an A-6 popped him with a rocket.

Maceo's wife starts wincing as we get deeper and deeper into talking shit. I ask her if we are bothering her.

"It is important that Maceo has other vets to talk to, but why do you keep going on about this?" I try to stop but Maceo keeps going.

"This is important, we must never forget this," he says. I see the pain on his wife's face. It is clear she too must wear this legacy of his. I stumble home about 1:30 AM.

The special rum Maceo served was good, I guess—no hang over. This morning we go through Havana and out beyond to where Hemingway kept his boat on the Rio Tarara, and what was once a youth recreation camp. In the good old days before the collapse of the Soviet Union Cuba could afford a year-round camp for children. Kids got R & R free. The elaborate facilities are now mostly abandoned, sections near the Marina are rapidly undergoing conversion to tourist facilities, but a section is being used for children from Chernobyl.

Apparently, Fidel is a sucker when it comes to children. The story is that when Fidel visited Kiev a mother of a sick child from Chernobyl asked him if he would help them. Whether he was drinking or not at the time is not known, but he did promise. So far almost 14,000 kids suffering diseases directly or indirectly related to the Chernobyl accident have received medical treatment. The average stay is 45 days, but some have remained over two years. Kids either come with a parent or in small groups. While the facilities are humble by our standards, they are truly paradise to the kids.

I watched a Cuban man of strong African heritage lovingly caressing a small blond Russian child. Cubans are obsessed with children. The workers there effuse a gentleness that could not have been put on.

The real subversion performed by the Cubans is not the medical treatment, but the music. It blows me away to watch blond kids perform for us. Though they lack the inherent rhythm of the Cubans, they dance salsa, rumba, cha-cha, and mambo. They get some of us old vets to dance with them. I'm afraid it's too late for most vets to get rhythm. I of course am an exception. I could not keep my tears from falling as the impact of the show found its way into my heart. And even now as I write this my tears are flowing.

There is a resort at the Marina Tarara, a nice beach, new facilities, and open port with berth rentals of only $.20 per foot, water and power included. Two bedrooms rent for $60-76. The people are so courteous.

Talk about being fucking wired. This mother fucker is fried. Jesse is from Boston, did Nam with the Army and a tour in Leavenworth. He moves in the upper torso. His hands flash out, sideways up, never down—like he's swatting quickly at bees coming on. He gesticulates like he's squeezing at something. His eyes seem to pop out or flutter while he stutters with a guttural voice and spits his thoughts or lack of thought out. He frequently goes off on tangents. He jumps in and out of conversations and homes in on anyone who will listen. His laughter is a closing of the eyes to slits, and he jerks like he's starting to sneeze. He's got a 25-foot sailboat. He wanted to know if I'd like to join him on a trip from Boston to Cuba. Yeah right! Like I'm going to sea with this crazy mother fucker.

"I don't think so Jesse," I say.

"No, no, no, no," he pops. "I don't fucking drink when I go to sea," he explains. Boy that's encouraging isn't it. "I might smoke pot, but no booze. No booze." Whoopee.

I get really fucked up, fucked up big time. I have not been this fucking wasted since the reunion in D.C. Get to bed around 6 AM. Miss the morning trip to the agriculture farm where they're doing research. The afternoon meeting with the Veteran chief, some Admiral, is a waste. God damn fucking vets spouting off horseshit. The Americans, not the Cubans. Laid down again in the afternoon, couldn't sleep. I'm ready to go home. Just tired.

I stop at Maceo's and have coffee, make small talk, then go out and stand by the ocean for a while and watch and feel. I don't know what it is about such times at the sea. When I stand and gaze out- ward and feel myself changing. Only this time the feeling is not a ponderous or profound sense that I am in transition. This time I feel more a quiet sense of resolve. That whatever it is that's coming is coming and I might as well relax and enjoy as much as possible.

We meet the Chinese Association. There are only about 700 born in China Chinese in all of Cuba. The total population is around 100,000 of mix Chinese/Cuban. Their four-page weekly is printed on a press built in 1906. Lead characters in boards in rows along the wall, hand worked press. It's weird to see Chinese talk in Cuban, gesturing like Cubans. They put sugar in their tea. A sin.

They're rehabbing an old building with small rooms that once had been a quirky hotel for couples who wanted to have sex in privacy since most homes were too crowded. Now it's going to become an old man's home. The guys get to live out their final years in the place of their fondest times when they were young. Karma lives.

Our farewell party is at a beautiful mansion some guy built in 1926 for his mistress. It was the friendship house the Soviets occupied when they were in Cuba. On a garden patio I sit with David from Alabama with an accent to match. I sit with Esmeralda and two Cuban vets. One guy joined Castro in the Sierra Maestra's when he was 17 years old. By the time he was 18, he was a first lieutenant. Spent three years in

Angola. He has soft white hair and a penetrating gaze. His buddy has the look of a vet also.

Through Esmeralda he says words to the effect,

"You cannot imagine the magnitude of our (veteran challenge) actions for them. It is something we shall never forget." Jesus Christ, we're fucking nobodies, and they're treating us like national heroes.

• • • •

Honolulu May 1998

ON HAWAIIAN AIRLINES Flight 11 to Honolulu for the second time in a month. Listening to Israel Kamakawiwo'ole on a CD. Had planned on keeping this a travel journal. Note it's been used twice so far. First for my trip to Nicaragua in '88 then Cuba in '95. A lot of water has run under my bridge in the 10 years.

February '88 I remember Sue and I parted at San Francisco Airport. She went to San Diego. She was thin-thin and had "the look" by then. Cuba was a free trip. This is in a way like the other two trips, a journey of peace. Last one was Dad's colon surgery. This one Mom and a stroke. Thought I had everything worked out. Planning is for shit. The gods always decide. Mom so full of hope about a new lease on life doing exercises, then bam. Have no idea what I'll be faced with when I get there. My inclination is to stop the move to the west coast. I feel morbid, but I just don't see much more time for Mom. I don't even know if I want to ask her to fight anymore. If she gives up it will be the same spiral as Uncle Sunny and Auntie Rose. Have got to focus on Dad too, see that he doesn't get depressed.

I'm pretty good about all this shit. I do not feel imposed on. This is just family. In a way I'm thankful for having the opportunity to say my goodbyes slowly rather than have them go fast like Dad almost did in '81. I guess the gods have been kind to me.

Crying as I write this. I always wanted wisdom. From the time I can remember I wanted to know, to understand. I never was or am a book person. I always needed to experience. And I have. Betty said to me first thing after reading my latest draft of "the novel."

"You do death good!"

"You mean well," I answered.

"No, good," she responded. Well, no shit Dick Tracy. I've done it and seen it enough, I don't just have the T shirt, I got the whole mother fucking franchise.

Speaking of the novel, wonder when I'll get to it again. Thought I had it this last go around, and I got too much negative feedback. So, it's back to the ole re-write again. God I was feeling so good about plowing into it, then this trip.

Well, who am I to question the will of the gods? I really do believe, I ain't just bull shitting. There are the gods, karma or whatever. I still need a little more work on not projecting into the future. I've never been one to piss in the past, but boy did I waste a fucking ton of time planning and strategizing about the future. I can't really think of any of them that bore fruit.

I can only recall two "visions" or inner enlightened moments that transpired. The first came when I was on a noon day run during my shipping days. I was between the terminal along the road by the Oakland Army base. "The voice" said my salvation from the life I detested would come via litigation. And it happened. I sued the fucks and got out of the business. Sued everybody that fucked me or with me. My apartment OOCL. Jerry. My condo I owned for a while. The bitch who fucked with me in the vocational rehab school I went to that the VA paid for. I think I did six or seven small claims or full lawsuits. Won every one of them. Then, when I was in debt big time, tapped out on credit cards. Rolling debt from old ones to new ones. The voice said, "Money is not the issue." I was still scared, but the voice was right. I got the VA 100% pension.

As I write this Israel is singing "Over the Rainbow," my favorite song of his. Magic, fucking magic. I do believe. I think the biggest change for me is that I am now truly fearless. This is the enchilada of life. I mean what the fuck can life throw at me. I've already accepted Mom and Dad going. What I've got to keep focused on is to stay in the moment. Right now. Make now as good as I can. I'm replaying "Over the Rainbow." I just wish I could be in this moment forever. Wonder if this means my time is short?

Finally got up the courage, or whatever just before I left Honolulu on the last trip to go up to Punchbowl. Finally visited French Deschaine's grave. 30 years after he got KIAed. Looked up Littler's grave and I'll be damned if he wasn't just four over from Frenchy and on the same line.

Littler and I were the only two from our PLC group to be commissioned. I'm the only one to survive. Saw him once up at Khe Sanh. He was flying CH-46's. We didn't speak. He tried to "convert" me to the Mormon faith when we were in transit at Treasure Island on the way back from summer PLC. Think it was '64? I made some sarcastic remarks.

Last time I interacted with Frenchy, I hit him with a can of fried ham. He was out sunning himself during the siege. Boy if looks could kill. Where in the fuck am I going with this? Time to put the pen down.

Noted a good-looking stewardess eye flirting with me. Good looking local girl. Probably mostly guava, Portuguese. Single, at least no ring. This is the longest I've been monogamous. Sue's condition cured me of that part of my past. Funny how I learn what's important. Like living guilt free. But I still have "it" I guess. I can still appreciate women and being attracted to and by them.

KD Lang is singing sexy "fuck me, fuck me" type songs and this stew keeps giving me these kissy face looks. I just smile my subtle smile. Look right into her eyes.

Last night at dinner Pat says she's afraid some "wild blonde" will get me.

"Why a blonde," I answer. "Why not a brunette?" and she goes, "Right, it could be a blonde, red head, or brunette." Wonder about women's premonitions. Here's this good-looking brunette giving me "the look." Fuck it. I got my share. She just went by again and gave me a sweet smile. This is more than just service.

Put in a Keali'i Reichel and he's singing a beautiful love song of some type. God am I in a romantic mood. Never thought when I was a young skirt chaser that I'd be filled with love at this age. I thought 55 years was when it was over. Hope I'm this romantic 30 years from now. Maybe my psyche is just helping to distract me from what's coming.

How different these feelings now compared to when I flew into Vietnam. Then my image of what I thought I wanted, so out of sync with what happened to and for me. Now, I know I'm doing it the right way. I'll follow my heart. Then, I listened to my head and my head was all fucked up. Amazing how far I've come.

Reminds me of when I was involved in the shit out at the Concord Naval Weapons Station. There was this old guy, Abraham Zwickle. I think he was 88 in 1987. He was a Jew who belonged to the Walnut Creek Unitarian Church and a practicing Zen. He was a conscientious objector during WWII, spent his jail time working with epileptics. They considered them mental retards then. Anyway, one day out at the tracks a Jewish peace group asked Abraham to speak to them. He tells them about him being a Jew who goes to a Unitarian church and practices Zen.

"I guess you can say I'm a backsliding Jew," he says. Then he introduces me. Tells them that I am a man who is passing in one lifetime from a warrior to enlightenment. Wonder how he knew? I certainly never tooted my horn. In fact, mostly stayed silent and rarely spoke there at the tracks.

Reality is a mother fucker. All the shit I took in the Marines being part Gook ends up paying off in the long run. I know that fact helped enormously in the VA giving me 100%. A good officer in Vietnam. Yeah, tough point to argue. Like I so totally realize the gods do indeed love me. What was a curse has become a badge of honor. Humility has never been a strong suit of mine. I am most proud of my standing among the gun fighters.

I gotta quit. Get ready for Mom and reality. Can't believe I've written this much. I miss my writing. It's been a long while since I've done this.

* * * *

Words 1999

I HAVE HEARD IT SAID that less than 20% of what we say to others is comprehended or remembered. It is not so much the words themselves than it is the intonations and connotations we use and perceive while communicating that matter. Language is my trade. From the time I was a child I have been repeatedly told how wonderfully I spoke. I have the gift of gab. A few years ago, while lecturing on a cruise ship about writing a woman came up to me and said: "You are so unusual. You are a writer who can speak beautifully."

I remember as a boy of four or five riding in a car with aunts and uncles. They were discussing a film called House of Horrors that Aunt Mary had just seen. She was relating the fear it induced in her.

"I'd like to live in a whore house," I interjected. The laughter roared in the car as soon as I said that. "What?" I innocently asked.

I notice that women live to use words, to talk. Communication of the live variety is for many of them essential. For them they are keeping it real. When I was doing my peace-activist gig a prescient woman said: "Ernie does not do small talk."

In the winter of 1999, I live for five months in a fully furnished luxury apartment looking out at the North side of Mount Shasta. My unit is beside the first hole of a golf course. The man who owns it rents it out in the winter for a low price. The summer days crowded with golfers and parties has given way to cold and silence.

Sharp freezing winds often buffet the cabin and shake the large plate glass sliding doors that frame Mount Shasta and its quiet surroundings. Short clumps of madrone bush, sage and wild grasses make up the countryside. I feed the wild birds off the back porch. I toss a large can of wild bird seed upon the brown winter grass. A fifty-pound bag of mixed seed costs less than fifteen dollars. The bag feeds hundreds of birds for over a month. For that small price I have company that does not intrude, but instead gives me pleasure. On bright sunny days I open the doors to the porch, and they sing for me. Words of gratitude and contentment, they whistle and chirp in harmony. Black tail deer gingerly walk unafraid across the course each early morning.

I am taking my sixth crack at doing my novel that I started in 1985. The novel is still not finished, but I do some beautiful writing while there.

While at Shasta I have the good fortune to be near the artist Dennis Smith who is also a Khe Sanh Marine. Dennis personally designed and built the Living Memorial Sculpture Gardens. It is eleven miles north east of the tiny California town of Weed alongside the road to Klamath Falls, Oregon. He lives on site in a tiny cabin with no running water or toilet.

Dennis works with fire and steel. Smitty was an artist from the time he was a child. His teacher noticed at an early age that he drew pictures with an astute eye and hand. He settled on metal sculpture after Vietnam. Fire and steel is what we endured at Khe Sanh, metal rounds exploding all around us for 76 days. I hate fireworks. I had to put up with that for too long. There is a world of difference between watching something and having to be in it. I was a bull's eye for too many real, not paper made, huge explosions.

Smitty uses an acetylene torch and steel rods for framing and torch cut metal plates to craft unique, beautiful things, animal, and human. His centerpiece at the Garden stands forty-five feet, human figures reaching for the sky. When I ask the meaning of the work, he says in his cigarette made deep baritone, "Buddha (his nickname for me) they are reaching for peace and salvation."

I remember a day while visiting him. He sits in his armchair that is set on a file cabinet high above me in filthy jeans and plaid wool shirt. His boots well aged, point to me. I lay upon his shoddy, cloth couch with my hands behind my head that rests upon a dirty cushion. In that position I have a clear view of him. He removes from the shelf beside him my book, Welcome To Vietnam, Macho Man. I know he has read it many times. He opens it.

"Listen to this, Buddha," he says. After a long draw from his cigarette, and exhaling he begins. It is the passage titled "The Locals." Like me his voice is that of a baritone. Mine is finer and softer, his deeper and richer. I am clean-shaven dressed in clean jeans and wool shirt. Dennis is a mountain of a man. Six feet five inches, bulky, not fat, with hair from head and face that covers what was no doubt once that of a handsome, darkhaired man. We both could be professional narrators if given the opportunity. His diction is precise, and he hits each word of the passage in perfect synchronization. When he finishes reading it he closes the book, begins nodding his head rapidly in agreement and goes: "Errrrrr... Buddha you sculpt with words." He then asks me my favorite passage from the book.

"The Stream." I answer without hesitation. "Why," he asks?

"Because it is the closest I came to doing poetry. You have questions, no doubt while reading 'The Locals,' do you not? You either get 'The Stream,' or you don't. Poets are the purest wordsmiths, in my opinion."

"Right on." He replies gesticulating his head in agreement once more while stroking his strong, large right hand over his flowing beard, contemplating what I just said.

"They are the ones who suffer the most, as artists aren't they?" As soon as I ask him, he again nods in agreement, then seems to come alive.

"The world does not understand what our art entails do they?" He pauses and intently stares down.

After taking a long, slow drag upon my cigarette, I harshly exhale and say: "Fuck them, Smitty. They would if they could. All they can do is admire, or more often criticize us. But, make no doubt about it, they envy us more than admire." He lets out a long staccato string of laughter.

"Come on Buddha. Let's have a beer," he pleads. He grips his armrests preparing to rise.

"Dennis. You know I don't go there anymore if I can help it. It doesn't work for me. It only works me."

"Yeah. Yeah. I know Buddha," he replies in resignation, slumps deep into his padded armchair. We quietly smoke the rest of our cigarettes without words being spoken. None are needed. They would have only gotten in the way. Our art is a lonely calling. Not solitary, but downright lonesome.

I often visit Dennis after my morning ritual of writing. Dennis is in a dry spell. His half-finished Iwo Jima monument stands, dust covered, in the center of his cabin.

It is now finished and in place, but when I knew Smitty, he hated it. He did not want to do that piece. He only did it to please those who were supporting him at the time.

Before he got his VA pension Dennis was destitute. People of the town of Weed and its surroundings supported Dennis, financially and with things like fresh water, propane, food, and wood for his cast iron stove. His fans who had money were the men of the local Kiwanis's club, and the Marine Corps League. Most were of our father's generation. WWII.

While I am there, I bring him to my place once a week for a hot bath and take him out afterwards for a good restaurant meal. I take him shopping for necessities and pay, but never for his cigarettes or beer. God does he drink and smoke. He always has a beer and cigarette in hand.

Dennis was born and raised as a Mormon. It was at Khe Sanh that he started smoking and drinking.

"Buddha, during the siege, I went from being a nonsmoker to four packs a day," he says. Entrails of smoke from his cigarette play as they rise beside the fire of his open cast iron stove. The light of morning through the glass window lights the rising smoke and gives it a hue of light brown. I also am smoking. I quit in 1974 and only recently took up the habit again. I can understand why Dennis took up the habit of tobacco and alcohol. He uses the best things at hand to try to deal with his stress.

Now, the cigarettes and booze help little and greatly harm him. His father is a dentist. He visits Dennis once a year at the site. He extracts Dennis's rotting teeth. His smoking, drinking and lack of cleaning have caused him to have gum disease. Dennis does not take care of himself. He does not give a shit about anything except his art and booze.

I am doing good art. He is stuck. Only a fellow artist can understand the frustration of not being able to do one's craft.

His chair stands upon a metal file cabinet four feet off the floor. He does this so that he can look out his large front window at those who might be visiting the Garden. The chair is high up in order to see if anyone comes down the narrow dirt road that leads to his cabin. He oftentimes runs out back and hides from visitors, both known and not. That is a recluse. I am a man living a life of solitude, then and now. I love and respect him, but better him than me. His life is only his art. Everything else whether material or human is extraneous for him.

He will probably die a drunk. He will not be remembered for that. His great art will last as long as it is maintained, and even when left untended it will still take many lifetimes to rust away. He gives away more art than he sells. The one he makes the most copies of is the one called running man. It is open. It is an outline of a man in flight made from very thin welding rods.

I have five of his original statues. One is a sitting Buddha that he created using barbed wire that he bent into shape with his hands before painting it black. When handing it to me he says:

"Buddha this is how I see you. I will never make another."

People I don't know send me handmade and bought art because they are so moved by my book. I have two custom-made, fine-grained, wood handled knives. Smitty sees one and comments on its quality. Smitty knows better than me such things.

Hotel Ceci 2000

Journal Entry

DECEMBER 21 It's almost 7 PM. I'm propped in bed in a $24 a night room in San Jose Los Cabos, Mexico. What a way to start my R & R. Dad died nine days ago and it was a pisser. Got a free plane and condo trip from Paul. I feel so alone now without dad. I'll never see or hear him again. A TV and loud air conditioner is blocking out the world outside. I had a long, lonely lunch earlier. In the center of town. Solonika—some fucking expensive place. Three glasses of wine, sandwich, coffee and cobbler was almost 500 pesos. My room was 180. Used to eat 25 cent tacos on the road to Ensenada when I was in high school circa 1959-60. Got sick too.

Alone in a dingy room is a proper way for me to start my goodbye to Daddy. He was such a cheap shit, at times. Pinched the pennies. Left me $120,000 or so. Tomorrow I get a $350 a night condo in Cabo San Lucas called Finistera for free. Dad would like that too.

What am I going to do with the rest of my life? Now, that it is mine? The last few years. Shit, the last few years? Since Nam, I've been living (?) my life for my family. Evie, my parents. Now what? What will I become now? I know that I will evolve. I am ready to settle down and write. I don't need more. A quiet, peace- ful place and a pen. But I don't want to be alone.

I just have to kill tonight, then hopefully get a cab out of here around 1 PM. Check out time. Maybe I'll grab a bite at a restaurant on the block. Forgot Pepto Bismol.

Started to read Alfredo Vea, *The Gods go Begging.* Started well, then drags. Descriptive prose is best done in small doses. Novel is like a long mural. A picture, a piece, a scene. Castlerock will be that, a two part mural. Someday. If I live long enough. It went on forever because I now see that it was necessary. I wasn't ready.

The muse has been very generous in the last couple of months. I don't know how much will be used if any, but I did some good stuff. Clear, clean copy. I did some of the stuff right off the top of my head. Bang. Minutes for an entire scene. Setting, dialogue. Wow. It impressed me.

I felt so serene, not excited as I wrote the scenes. My voice felt clear, concise. It was as though I watched the movie. As though it was given to me. Some sort of a gift, or retribution, perhaps, for my suffering. The pain in my back, hip and right leg merely reminds me of the ache in my heart I cannot yet face. My Daddy is gone. My heart is broken. I will always remember him. Fondly.

Te Amo, the old black mother says on the TV showing the Discovery channel. Black dude, his throat cut. A US Trauma Center documentary. All black guys with gunshot wounds. One dumb fuck, young white guy, face fucked up. Bragging about getting his ass kicked. Stitched his face, checked him out, still drunk. The nurse laughing it off. America the Beautiful. Chopper flying in shot up or crashed into guys. Young mostly. Survival. Young Hispanic woman. Her tits blurred out, but the long, serrated kitchen knife in her chest graphically displayed. Proper taste, I guess. American TV too much, even in Español.

Left for a drink just before 9. One margarita, side order of wonderful guacamole, chips greasy, but good. No doubt long fried in liquid lard, rendered from reluctant, gaunt beef cattle somewhere in arid Mexico. The margarita came in a glass goblet that could do a communion in an Italian parish. Paul was right though. Their drinks are watered down. Lots of frozen stuff, not much tequila. Paul knows his booze. Watched him drink a fifth of Black Jack and two doubles at dinner one night, all inside of 5 hours. Watched him fall down, too. Same with Pat, watched her fall down ass drunk too. Too many times.

Glad she did, takes a lot of shit to get me to go, when I feel owing to someone. Now I don't owe anyone anything.

Thought about my latest flame Ellen while I sat along a back wall, alone, in the Jasmine Restaurant. At a nice table with fucking birds in a big cage next to me, singing away to Mexican love songs. One lone American couple leave. I watch middle aged Americans, hand-in-hand, stroll by the quiet, narrow side street, right outside the picture windows and open doorway entrance. Now, three stoic waiters to serve only me. I drink from the Holy Grail through a straw. I'd take my shoulder out if I had to hoist the fucker every time I sipped.

A withered faced smiling dark Indian featured guy with straw Compesino hat and colorful serape stopped and chatted with two of the waiters at the entrance. He held bouquets of roses, red. Three to a bunch. I thought of Ellen and if she were here, I would have bought some for her. And I don't do flowers.

Alone now, in this still room. The TV from the front lobby is loud. My room—two doors in. Two guys yakking in Spanish that echoes down the hall. Outside, near buildings of various tenancy, ring to the clammer of the passing night. I hear the cars that rumble and roar by. It is better with the roar of the air conditioner/fan on. No—it's too fucking loud.

Feel like a shower, but it's too much. Shower is part of the bathroom, same floor, drain, toilet with seat, sink. Metope for a window. Small bare light bulb room. Separate bathroom with closing door. Didn't even look in the closet. Big mirror on old table. Across from my bed against the opposite wall and right ass next to an old fucking Samsung 12,000 BTU unit. Sounds like a Korean made thing. Loud.

I got on a Korean made T-shirt my sister brought me back from Korea. I babysit Dad for 2 weeks and I get this T-shirt. Never wore it before. Strange, the way symbols unfurl before one's eyes.

Ellen wouldn't mind this room for a night. She's done 3rd world, this is luxurious. She'd love walking around this old town. The shops, the quaint ambience. Pat would have shit a ton of bricks if I brought her to this place. Finistera is fine, but not the hotel Ceci I'm in now. Maybe that's one of the reasons I love and admire Ellen. She's unpretentious.

I hope we can connect, get in sync. If she'd just slow the fuck down and smell the roses for a while. Get off that speed kick she's hooked on.

Watching the Discovery channel again, this one on mines, lost limbs, 3rd world. Answer to detecting is in chemistry, I guess. Don't know Spanish. Plants, jellyfish. Microbiologist yakking away. Now state of the art wheelchair stories from Ipswich, England. Chairs that cost a car and with full attendants for the near paralyzed kid. While kids nearby shit worms and eat tortillas. It is beyond 2000. I'd turn it off, but I can't stand the silence right now. God, I'm so alone.

December 22 Went for a long walk around town this AM. Most shops don't open till 10:00. Ate breakfast at a nearby hotel. Sat beneath a mango tree on the patio and had great eggs, hash browns, fried beans, salsa, toast, pastries, coffee. Watched a couple my age. Blended families, two each, preteen to early teens. Look like a new couple. Their affection still new. The woman reached out and rubbed the arm of the guy after they ate. Thought of Ellen and how much I wish I could have been sitting with her and eating breakfast. How different I would have felt. Connected instead of alone.

I just realized. This will be my first Christmas all alone. Where I know no one else. Christmas is a lonely time anyway. Has been for me. Years of trying to satisfy others at Christmas. Family. Girlfriends. Scheduling time for each. No wonder I grew to hate it. Now, it doesn't matter, so it seems. I wonder if I'll get it back. Those everyday normal feelings. To feel fine just being OK. I have the financial means now to travel and write. All I want is someone to relax with, laugh with and love. I have my work and more than I'll ever finish (in my head) in my life. Five years is a lifetime for me to wait. I've been waiting so long.

December 23 Finistera Resort Got here at 1 PM and had to wait until 4 for my room. Sat out by the pool and drank Tecate beer and sucked limes in the sun. Big mistake. As a slow internal fog filled me with whatever, the loneliness set in. Couples together my age or older. Or couples with kids.

This place is up on the side of a cliff and you take an elevator up from the beach. In the elevator a tall roly-fat Japanese with long stringy wet hair joined us as we walk across the arch to my wing.

"That's the Blue Marlin Restaurant," the bellboy said.

Paul had told me not to eat there. "The foods awful," he claimed.

The fat Japanese guy, who by his walk I have ascertained is probably gay, goes, "That place will absolutely destroy your taste buds for Mexican food anywhere back in the States." He is gay and I wondered who to believe. Paul, an alcoholic with questionable taste, or some Japanese gay guy who doesn't give a shit about what he looks like? Paul's spent a lot of time in Mexico. This gay guy might live in Ft. Wayne, Indiana where a taco is as common as a luau.

Went to bed early, no meal. Ellen called, a pleasant surprise. It broke momentarily my isolation. I'll go sit in the sun and try Alfredo again tomorrow.

December 24 Alfredo's book doesn't really do it for me. It's like he's forcing his descriptive prose with stuff he's read somewhere. Sun was nice. Breeze kept it pleasant.

I am very depressed. A slow quiet despair. I miss my dad. I guess I need to go through it. Paul called after midnight. It's an hour earlier for him. He was slurring drunk. Kept asking if "you having a great time?" Dumb fuck is an idiot when he's drunk. Maybe he forgot my dad just died. Great way to spend Christmas Eve, talking to a fucking drunk, telling me he wished he was with me having "a great time."

I'd had four beers the first day here, no more lush shit for me. I'll save them for very special occasions. I think I'll toast Daddy with a shot of Black Jack and a beer if I can get up the stomach for it.

Spent two hours in the sun. Walked the beach. Didn't go in. Too much undertow. You can tell with a steep banked beach that there's undertow. I'll go up to the Blue Whale Bar. Finish off Alfredo and go onto something I know I'll like even though I've read his stuff lots of times. Steinbeck. Zapata. Ellen got me the two for Xmas. I read a review of Vea's _Gods go Begging_ that was glowing. His Vietnam stuff was mostly overdone bullshit. Well maybe I'm wrong. He was a fucking doggie and they are fucked up far more than the Corps.

December 25 Talked to Ellen just after midnight. Best present I got. Watched the sun as a thin red line on the horizon grow and blacken the banks of clouds black to the back light. Then, the sky went light blue above it.

Overcast some, breezy. Lot of time in the sun; emotionally I feel like shit. I need to go home. I'm waiting at the airport for my flight back to the world. I hope this is my last solitary journey. I'm tired of being alone. I've been running in place, going nowhere all these years. An observer of life around me. A critical eye, whose heart is vacant of a sense of belonging. I want to open up, but I've been cut off so long, I fear I've forgotten how. What are we without some semblance of innocence? I am foolish often, but not innocent. I've been standing apart from a world that rejected me and I it. I've always wanted peace, since Nam, but have never found it. The Zen way does not work for I have been un- willing to detach from things. I am already dead and unwilling to let that reality set in, to live in the moment, I know I must accept that premise.

I saw this so clearly during the death of Daddy. All his questions leading up to his final decision to proceed. I remember the questions by Daddy to me. "Are you afraid of dying, son?"

"No," I said.

"Why not?"

"I guess cause I've seen so much Daddy, I've done so much, it no longer frightens or bewilders me."

Then he asked me the key question, "Am I going to die, Ern?"

"Yes," I said coolly as we looked at one another. Deep into one another's eyes. I shall never forget his look. First fright. Then, resignation. Little did I realize what a struggle it would be to accomplish my task. My mission. I was ruthless in getting Daddy what he wanted. People feared me. I got what I wanted. But at what price?

• • • •

Alone 2008

I SIT HERE ALONE ONCE again two months into my sixty-fifth year. My third marriage has ended. Writing of this nature is always painful for me. My beloved, late daddy told me that I write best when I write about that which I have personally experienced. Daddy told me he wished he could have been the man who I am.

Being a star is not easy. I have been one as long as I can remember.

It is not yet seven a.m. Chuck called my daughter Evie yes- terday and told her that he wants me to call him.

Who is Chuck? He is one of my closest Vietnam bred brothers. I call us the four horsemen of the Apocalypse. Chuck, Kenny Pipes, who I call Babe, and Fast Eddie Feldman. We bond forever while we desperately tried to try to stop the execution of Manuel Pina Babbitt, a Marine Khe Sanh vet none of us knew in Vietnam.

His state paid public defender discovers me because of my reputation and asks if I will help. I know full well when I ask Chuck, Kenny and Fast Eddie to join me that Manny is going to die. I could not live with myself if I do not. These men Chuck, Kenny and Ed are genuine, brave, gifted warriors. They have the talents I need for Manny.

It is most difficult for Kenny, my closest brother, but he comes onboard when I ask, just as Chuck and Fast Eddie do.

Chuck pays the greatest price in trying to save Manny. He loses his job. His firm spends over a million dollars in pro bono fees on Manny. Chuck respects me. Chuck fondly calls me Bubba. I know that I am the lesser man than any of the other three. My post-Vietnam job career attests to that.

Kenny is the bravest, most honorable Marine and person I have ever known. Fast Eddie Feldman, like Kenny, is a Silver Star recipient from Khe Sanh.

I am a star. A man's man.

I am an utter failure in relationships with women. I cannot live without them. They intoxicate me. I am addicted. Financially, women have cost me. But money loss pales in comparison to the pain and suffering I endure. It is always relationship according to them.

I cannot live that way. I do not cause any friction in my "relationships." I take responsibility for my actions. I keep my shit to myself.

I go to bed with Mary Poppins and wake up next to Dracula's wife.

· · · ·

December 12, 2009, 7:39:14 AM PST

BABE. HANG ON AND IN there my dearest brother. I, and whomever I might be with at that time (Ernesto is a rolling stone) will make this momentous "Chinggadero." Just gimme the time, place, and dress code. I'll even proudly wear dress blues, tennis shoes, and a light coat of oil.

As you said, there were only 36 of us (rifle company commanders) in the entire Marine division of 10,000. There weren't many of us to begin with. You and I are still standing (staggering). Though human and flawed, we are righteous, honorable men. What more can a man wish for in life? I'd thankfully take all the pain in my life that I've endured, over again, just to have stood and fought (literally) beside you. Sweet and pure this love we share that was forged on "the line." doing "gun-time." You personify what gunfighter really means. All gave some. You gave all Blackbud Bravo Six Actual.

Click your handset twice if all is secure. Ernesto

• • • •

Blackbud Delta Six Actual

MY BROTHER AND MOST Cherished Companion at Arms,

The honor you do me leaves me speechless. I know we have been through so much together and on some lonesome paths, on occasion, by ourselves. Still, we remain linked like the Native Americans that moved through our country long years ago, bound to each other in spirit and thought. Or, just perhaps, even further back in time; like two Roman Centurions on the far edges of the Empire—going into the fiery breach again and again, not for Rome—but for those that we lead into battle and for each other. Two of the Senior Centurions, 26th Maniple, 3rd Legion. Have we done this before?

I ramble. Just know that I am honored by your words and by your Friendship over all these years. I sometimes think of the far distant future with some trepidation; it just might be our des- tiny to do it again, on the wheel and road of life. If so, I will have your 6 as we, once again, deploy and move into the furnace of the battle field.

With Respect and Warmest of Regards. Ken
Black Bud Bravo 6, Actual

• • • •

New Year's Eve 2019

ENROUTE FROM SAN FRANCISCO to Hilo

It is early morning on the Grand Princess. From my private balcony I gaze out into a warm, overcast Pacific. There are no ships or other signs of life. Our bow waves and stern churnings mark my course. I love cruising on open seas. Time becomes meaningless on endless ocean.

Being an old restless soul, the sea, no matter its condition, comforts and relaxes me. I cruised frequently with daddy after mom died. The last was just three months before he let go for good. We slept like babies while skirting a typhoon.

It is almost two decades since daddy passed. I am Catholic raised and educated but follow Karma. Life is a journey back to the One. I am my father's loyal son.

• • • •

First Voyage Honolulu 1947 Aloha Tower

VIVID MEMORIES OF MY first voyage play. At the railing of a tramp steamer held in my father's arms I gaze down at four young Hawaiian boys treading water.

"Aloha, Aloha," they call like barking seals.

"It's custom," daddy says. The man standing beside us flips silver dimes to the excited boys. He's smoking a big cigar and is very fat. Each boy waits for his coin to hit the water before quietly sinking down into the black. Moments later the dark-skinned boy explodes out from the darkness, arm held high. White teeth shine above his big smile.

"Mahalo," the boy barks. Then puts the treasure in his mouth.

"That's where they keep their money," daddy says.

Passengers toss their lei onto the water as we pull away from the dock. The ship's horn sounds in long blasts.

"Why are they throwing them away, daddy?"

"It's custom," he says. "You'll learn. It is a Hawaiian custom." "Does everybody have customs, daddy?"

"Yes," he says and smiles. "Everyone."

. . . .

First Fright

I FEEL THE POWER OF the ocean as soon as we clear the harbor entrance. Gentle rolling quickly gives way to strange bouncing.

"We have to go below," Daddy says. "A big storm is coming." Between the islands of Maui and Hawaii ships bound for Hilo transit the dreaded Alenuihaha Channel. My only vivid memory of that part of our journey is a crewman bringing us life jackets and putting one on me. I feel like a chick in a shell of cork. When times were simpler, one size fit all.

. . . .

Captain Cook Hawaii 1951

ALMOST EVERY SUMMER when I am young, we vacation at the bay where Captain Cook was killed and eaten by the locals. Late one morning my cousin John and I watch the Hawaiians launch outrigger canoes.

"Come here when I get back. I give you kids fish," an old Hawaiian man says. John and I are wide-eyed, amazed at the scene playing out in front of us.

"What time?" I shout as he begins to paddle away.

"Watch da sun, boy." He points at Mauna Kea. "Tell time wit da sun and moon. No need clock. Watch da ocean. I going come in when da tide change."

We play along the lava field that lines the inner cove. We can see their canoes across the bay, near the monument to Cook. They fish with hand lines. With an outgoing tide they make their way back to the landing cove. The young men land their canoes first so they can assist the elders. Our guy must have been among the oldest because all he had to do was get out. Two young bucks hoisted his canoe and carried it up on shore.

"Go get me some coconut leaf," he says to me, nodding at a young tree nearby with low hanging branches.

"You want me to pull off a branch?"

"Eh kid, where your brain?" he says. "Just pick two stems for carry da fish. Hurry up. Fish getting old." John and I race back to our summer cottage with three fish each, so fresh they still have their bright coloring.

As mom opens the door to the back kitchen, I shout out: "Look what the Hawaiians gave us."

• • • •

Harry Truman 1952

MY COUSIN JOHN AND I are crabbing at the bridge just before you turn off into the Kaneohe Marine Corps Air Base. I see a big black Cadillac convertible with its top down coming at us from Kailua. As it nears, I notice the guy in back is wearing an all- white outfit, hat to match. As it nears it slows because of the narrow bridge. The two guys in front are in dark suits.

"It's President Truman," I yell. He smiles his big grin and waves at me. The admiral in back with him is laughing. With the back of their heads showing as they pass into history John asks, "Who's dat?"

Don't miss out!

Visit the website below and you can sign up to receive emails whenever Ernest Spencer publishes a new book. There's no charge and no obligation.

https://books2read.com/r/B-A-VKJU-OBUZB

BOOKS2READ

Connecting independent readers to independent writers.

Also by Ernest Spencer

Macho Man
Welcome Home, Macho Man - A PTSD Life

Watch for more at https://www.corpsproductions.org.

About the Author

Ernest Spencer is a Hawaiian born Korean American. Born in the mid 1940's, he joined the Marine Corps Reserve in 1963.

During his second year in college, where he was studying philosophy, he "was overwhelmed by the futility of reason as an effective force in life." Disillusioned by reason, his life did not make sense to him. He was drawn to the Marine Corps by the sense of belonging. The Corps also offered him the chance to confront life rather than read about it. Spencer states, "I could confront life by going to the edge, or at least what I perceived as the edge: Existence itself."

In 1967, he was sent to lead a line unit (an infantry unit) that is at Khe Sanh, the 1st Battalion, 26th Marine Regiment. There were four rifle companies in this infantry battalion: Alpha, Bravo, Charlie, and Delta. Spencer commanded Delta. He recalls "you have got to understand what it means to a 24-year-old guy who's macho to be made a commanding officer of a rifle company in combat. He is Jesus Christ himself." He was also the first Korean American to command a marine rifle company in combat.

Since his time in Vietnam, Spencer founded a publishing company.

Now, after enjoying retirement, he has founded a non-profit to support education in his beloved Hawaii. He is now writing a historical fiction trilogy and self-narrating his books for the audio book market.

And keeping his softball skills up!

Read more at https://www.corpsproductions.org.

www.ingramcontent.com/pod-product-compliance
Lightning Source LLC
Chambersburg PA
CBHW072221150726
48002CB00005B/1915